THE RELUCTANT EVANGELIST

Embrace Your Gifts
and Fulfill God's Purpose

dave kachele

xulon PRESS

Table of Contents

Introduction

C an you identify with the title? If so, you are in good company. Statistics reveal that about 95%* of believers do NOT have evangelism (telling others the Salvation Message) as a dominant gift. This is a 50-Day journey *designed to inspire, encourage, and equip ALL of us* to share the message **when God gives the opportunity**. The goals of this 50-Day journey (7 weeks and a day) are:

- To **deepen** your **relationship** with God,
- To **increase** your **understanding** of how God made you, and
- To **show** you how to **focus your gifts** on fulfilling God's purpose.

What is God's purpose? He simply wants to be in a relationship with every man, woman, boy, and girl. Jesus stated it clearly in **The Great Commission:** *"All authority in heaven and on earth has been given to Me. Therefore, go and make disciples of all nations, baptizing them in the name of the Father and of the Son and of the Holy Spirit, and teaching them to obey everything I have commanded you. **And surely I am with you always, to the very end of the age.**"* (Mt 28: 18-20) The question is: *"How can I do my part in fulfilling the Great Commission with **my own** God-given gifts?"* Perhaps you've put it differently: *"How can I do my part in winning souls and growing disciples, and still be comfortable in my own skin?"* **Jesus included the promise of His presence. His strength, wisdom, words, and timing come with it.**

THE RELUCTANT EVANGELIST: Embrace Your Gifting and Fulfill God's Purpose has two sections:

Section I: FEEDING THE SPRING

Jesus stood and said in a loud voice, "If anyone is thirsty, let him or her come to Me and drink. Whoever believes in Me as the Scripture has said, streams of living water will flow from within in him." By this He meant the Spirit, whom those who believed in Him were to receive. (John 7:37-39) The first three weeks of this journey will remind you of your preciousness to God. You have put your trust in Jesus and the mercy and grace of God. That same trust assures you of your immense value that is not based upon your performance but God's demonstrated love. (Rom 5:8) You will get a handle on how God made you with your own spiritual gifts, personality, and passion. Finally, it will help you to think deeply about your ongoing relationship with the Lord.

Section II: LETTING THE LIVING WATER FLOW

In your heart set apart Christ as Lord. Always be prepared to give an answer to everyone who asks you to give the reason for the hope that you have. But do this with gentleness and respect. (1 Pe. 3:15) This section contains a simple way of sharing the gospel in a relational way as God opens doors to do so. It's not about being obnoxious or confrontational. It includes how to work within your own community of believers. There is also a week devoted to cults, other religions, and hard questions. Week 7 will help with discipling a new believer.

Each day begins with a story. I hope you enjoy this one:

We were at a Mariners game in Seattle. Our two boys had just dropped their gloves into Mom's lap and headed for the snack bar. As they reached the end of the aisle, Enrique Wilson hit a foul that had Dona's name on it! **My wife plays catch by covering her head**! She sank deeper and deeper into her seat and looked up to see a frame of hands. In the center was a white dot that was getting larger every second! One of those hands was mine. I one-handed that ball without dropping the sunflower seeds out of my other hand! Dona let out her held breath. Instantly, I became famous in our section. My first thought was, "Big deal. I caught a foul ball." But as they continued I got into it! "OK, cool! It wasn't a home run hit by Ken Griffey, Jr. but hey, what are the odds?!"

The foul ball is thinking that only 5%(ChurchGrowth.org) of us can be personally involved in sharing the Gospel. Do you "play catch by covering your head" when the door opens to share the gospel? You've prayed for a loved one to come to know Christ. That's God's passion for souls! Let's turn that foul into a HOME RUN!

As you read each day, write down your own thoughts. In 50 days, you, perhaps a reluctant evangelist now, will be better able to **embrace your gifts and fulfill God's purpose.**

Contact Dave Kachele: www.winandgrow.com WinNGrow@gmail.com
626-905-2893 Win and Grow on Facebook Twitter LinkedIn

Acknowledgements

I have been blessed with family, friends, and mentors all of my life. I am deeply grateful to the Lord Jesus for each one. They have shown grace, patience, love, and wisdom in their interaction with me. I cannot mention you all, but THANK YOU from the bottom of my heart.

My wife, **Dona Kachele** has been my faithful companion and wise mentor for over 39 years. Win and Grow Ministries and *THE RELUCTANT EVANGELIST: Embrace Your Gifts and Fulfill God's Purpose* would have been nothing more than an unfulfilled dream without her.

Dr. John Trent, author of *THE BLESSING*, has been an amazing mentor and encourager. John sparked and re-ignited my passion to see this project through to its end. He also provided the LOGB® Personality Assessment and the idea of a new title—the one on the front of this book.

The following have supported me with encouragement, proof reading, prayers, and in other ways too numerous to mention: **John Fraley, Bob Tucker, Brad and Julie Townsend, Richard Kachele, Doctors Henry and Jan Harbuck and all the fellow ministers with the Association of Evangelical Gospel Assemblies (AEGA), Pastor Dale Winslow, his leadership team, and all of the family at Foothill Community Church, Doctor John Trent, Brandon Burton, Beth Swanson, Margaret Davis, Michelle Weaver, Eswin and Heather Rios, Jimmy and Lynda Stewart, and our friends at the Foothill Vista Bible Study which we've had the privilege of leading since 2004.**

I must also thank my pastoral leadership through the years: **The Brothers at Maranatha House; Pastors Mel Brewer, Mel Steward, Richard Carpenter, Allen Ratta, Darrell Elliott, John Glennon, Dale Winslow**, and many others who have helped me grow in the grace and knowledge of the Lord Jesus Christ.

Endorsements

"*THE RELUCTANT EVANGELIST: Embrace Your Gifts and Fulfill God's Purpose* is a challenging yet simple guide to share with friends, disciples and neighbors. **For the person who has a healthy fear of sharing Christ with others, Dave Kachele does a wonderful job of demonstrating and guiding them into a place of confidence and peace.** Thank you, Dave, for writing such an outstanding resource!"
Dr. Rhonda Beckwith, Marriage & Family Therapist

"With **Win and Grow Ministries** and *THE RELUCTANT EVANGELIST: Embrace Your Gifts and Fulfill God's Purpose*, Dave Kachele has provided a tool for two groups: Any who want to jump-start the discipline of listening to God and any who want to take the next step in radical obedience to Him. **Our church used it. I recommend it.**"
Dale Winslow, Sr. Pastor, Foothill Community Church, Azusa, CA

"Dave Kachele's *THE RELUCTANT EVANGELIST*, is an excellent tool for any Christian seeking to unleash their potential for reaching people for Christ. It will challenge readers to deepen their relationships with God and others and in the process, bear fruit that will last. Drawing from over thirty-five years of experience in ministry and Christian education, **Dave Kachele writes in a practical and approachable style, bringing a wealth of resources to your fingertips.** Having used this book myself with my adult small group in my church, I strongly recommend it to Christians who desire to grow in their faith while unlocking doors to personal evangelism."
Andy Fishbeck, Sr. Pastor, Sugar Grove Free Methodist Church, Terre Haute, IN

"We believe that Evangelical Christians need this book in their arsenal! *THE RELUCTANT EVANGELIST* **is a resource for spiritual growth, provides ammunition for defending the faith, and will help any Christian to be more comfortable sharing faith in Christ.** One dynamic section gives a concise summary of cults, other

religions, suggestions for handling difficult questions, and sharing with atheists and agnostics. It contains help for understanding and witnessing to these people."
Hank Bode, J. D., Vice President Emeritus, Azusa Pacific University
Sherri Bode, Assoc. Professor, 1978 - 2005- Azusa Pacific University

"I am pleased to endorse **Win and Grow Ministries** under the direction of Dave Kachele. The emphasis on making disciples is appropriate for the days in which we live, and will help churches refocus on their primary ministry. **Dave has a heart for evangelism and is well-equipped to guide believers toward becoming more able to share the Gospel.** Also of much help is *THE RELUCTANT EVANGELIST: Embrace Your Gifts and Fulfill God's Purpose*, a 50-Day devotional and study guide. Between Dave ministering personally in Christian communities and this resource, participants will come away challenged and encouraged to do God's work."
John Fraley, MBA, MA, Nonprofit Manager (Retired)

"Dave Kachele, in his love for sharing Christ, **offers effective intrapersonal keys** to discovering biblical direction in sharing the gospel with others, winning souls to Christ, and growing disciples."
Michael and Jovie Benavides, Directors of "Community Meal," Azusa, CA

"I sincerely hope that *THE RELUCTANT EVANGELIST: Embrace Your Gifts and Fulfill God's Purpose* reaches millions of believers because the wisdom, mercy and inspiration found in these pages has power to set reluctant evangelists free! **I believe through the instruction and encouragement of this devotional, many will be won to Christ!"**
Brandon Burton, layman and former student of Dave Kachele

Preview Lessons

Preview-Lesson 1

Why Are Most of Us "Reluctant Evangelists?"

"Evangelism" is simply communicating the Good News (Gospel) about Jesus Christ with the intent of helping someone else to know Him as you do.

C an you relate to the word "RELUCTANT" in the title? If so, you're in good company. The Spiritual Gift Survey found at churchgrowth.org reveals that only about 3% of laity and 5% of clergy have evangelism as a dominant gift.

Here's a story of a **"Bumbling Evangelist."** (From Day 26)

"A nice young couple lived around the corner from us. I just knew they needed to know Jesus so we invited them over for dinner with the purpose in mind of leading them to Christ. It was a long time ago, but I'm pretty sure they did pray the "sinner's prayer" before they <u>escaped</u>. Afterward however, we were never able to make contact again; a relationship never developed. If discipleship occurred, it was without our influence."

Spiritual mugging is not effective. Maybe you've heard stories like this or you've been on the receiving or giving end of an episode like the one above.

If you're part of a group doing this together, share your stories.

Besides hearing about, witnessing, or being involved in a "bumbling evangelist" episode, what hinders you from sharing the Gospel? Below is a list. Check all that apply.

- _____ I'm an introvert
- _____ I don't know what to say to someone about how to know the Lord.
- _____ I'm better at showing the love of God than talking.
- _____ I think showing God's love is better than just talking.
- _____ I don't know where to look in the Bible to explain the Gospel.
- _____ I'm afraid of being rejected or made fun of.
- _____ Other (below)

- _____

- _____

How did you come to know Jesus?

If you're part of a group, partner up with another person in the room and share your stories with one another. If not, tell your story to another believer this week.

Preview-Lesson 2

Why Shouldn't We Be "Reluctant" to Share the Gospel?

As fully devoted followers of Jesus Christ, disciples, the Bible is our "Manual for Life." In the Bible we find our Identity and our purpose in life. The apostle Peter summed them both up in one verse:

> ". . .You are a chosen people (person), a royal priesthood (priest or priestess), holy (set apart), a people (person) belonging to God, thatyou may declare the praises of Him Who called you out of darkness into His wonderful light."
> (1 Peter 2:9)

What else does the Bible say about helping others to come to know Jesus? Discuss these passages.

Matthew 22:36-40, Mark 12:29-31
"Teacher, which is the greatest commandment in the Law?" Jesus replied: "'Love the Lord your God with all your heart, . . . soul, . . . mind, . . . and strength.' This is the first and greatest commandment. And the second is like it: 'Love your neighbor as yourself.' All the Law and the Prophets hang on these two commandments."

Matthew 28:18-19
"Then Jesus came to them and said, "All authority in heaven and on earth has been given to Me. Therefore go and make disciples of all nations, baptizing them in the Name of the Father and of the Son and of the Holy Spirit, and teaching them to obey everything I have commanded you. And surely I am with you always, to the very end of the age."

Romans 10:13-15, 17
"Everyone who calls on the name of the Lord will be saved. How, then, can they call on the One they have not believed in? And how can they believe in the One of Whom they have not heard? And how can they hear without someone preaching to them? And how can anyone preach unless they are sent? So, faith comes from hearing the message, and the message is heard through the Word about Christ."

Acts 2:42, 47

"They devoted themselves to the apostles' teaching and to fellowship, to the breaking of bread and to prayer. . . . And the Lord added to their number daily those who were being saved."

1 Peter 3:15

"But in your hearts set apart Christ as Lord. Always be prepared to give an answer to everyone who asks you to give the reason for the hope that you have. <u>But do this with gentleness and respect.</u>

Write down your thoughts and those of others if you're part of a group:

Preview-Lesson 3

How Can We Overcome Our Reluctance to Share the Gospel?

Feed the Spring . . . Let the Living Water Flow. . . Feed . . .
(John, Chapter 4; 7:37-39)

"On the last and greatest day of the feast, Jesus stood and said in a loud voice, 'If anyone is thirsty, let him come to Me and drink. Whoever believes in Me, as the Scripture has said, streams of living water will flow from within him."

What gave Jesus boldness to yell this out?
He knew Who He was; He knew His purpose.

How can we overcome our reluctance to share His Gospel?

Feeding the Spring (Days 1-21)

First, we must fully accept who we are in Christ. You are **PRECIOUS** to God and a **PARTAKER** of His nature. Therefore, you have His **PASSION** and **PERSPECTIVE** to fulfill His **PURPOSE** with **PATIENCE, PEACE**, and **PERSEVERENCE.**

> "For you know that it was not with perishable things such as silver or gold that you were redeemed from the empty way of life handed down to you from your forefathers, but with the precious blood of Christ, a lamb without blemish or defect." (1 Peter 1:18-19)

What does the world say about your value? What do you say about your value?

- **Knowing your real worth is the 1st and most important key to overcoming your reluctance to sharing the Gospel when God opens the door.** (Days 1-7)
- **Understanding and accepting how God made you is the 2nd key.** (Days 8-15)
- **Your ongoing Jesus story is about living IN the amazing love of the Father! This is the 3rd key in your eternal spring.** (Days 16-21)

Letting the Living Water Flow (Days 22-50)

Once your God-given value is engrained, practice expressing His love to people.

> **". . .The only thing that counts is faith expressing itself through love." (Galatians 5:6b)**

"BUT WHAT DO I SAY?!?"

- RELAX. Be natural. Be relational. Be real. Abide in Jesus. Be oBEdient.
- Be ready to tell your own story in just a few minutes.
- Know the "4 Spiritual Laws": LOVE; SEPARATION; REMEDY; RESPONSE
- Remember that loving service opens doors to share the Gospel with words.
- Love. . .Pray. . .Love. . .Pray. . . . Remember that the Holy Spirit is always drawing.
- Know, pray for, and look for "God moments" within your Circles of Influence
- Work with and within community
- "Make It Happen" so you're ready for "Let It Happen" moments
- Be ready to disciple a new believer

Section I

Feeding the Spring

Week 1

Foundational Lessons from the Letter "P"

Day One:
God Says I Am Precious, so I Am!

*For you know that it was not with perishable things such as silver or gold that you were redeemed . . .but with the **PRECIOUS** blood of Christ . . .* (1 Pt 1:18-19)

I was about ten years old when Mom sent me to the store with a $50 bill: I don't know how I lost it, but I was afraid going home with the news and NO GROCERIES! When I told my mom, she said, "It's okay, honey; it's only money." She spent her whole life showing people how precious they were.

What really gives us value?
From whom do we accept value assessments?

When Jesus came up out of the water, the Father spoke from heaven. *"This is my Son, whom I love; with Him I am well pleased."* (Mt 3:17) Jesus had not yet begun His ministry: no preaching good news to the poor, no restoring sight to the blind, no feeding the multitudes, no cross and resurrection . . . no work. Yet His Father said He was well pleased with Him.

Jesus was once asked, *"What must we do to do the works God requires?"* His answer was simple and profound. *"The work of God is this: believe in the One He has sent."* (Jn 6:28-29)

His love is not conditional upon works.

Ask yourself, "What could I do (or not do) to add to (or take away from) the worth that God has already bestowed upon me by His redemption with the precious blood of His Son? Could I somehow diminish or add to the intrinsic value God has given me through the sacrifice of Jesus?" (Rom 5:8) **Performance based value must be nailed to the cross!** Look Failure in the face. . .smile. . .and rest in God's grace. This will allow you to learn to serve out of the rest that comes from Him. (Heb 4:9-11)

Open your Bible, go to John 3:16, and pray it inserting your name in the appropriate places: *For God so loved _____.* . . . Now, just stop for a moment. Bow your head and receive afresh (or, perhaps for the first time) the love of God, demonstrated to you through Jesus. Soak it in. **Our preciousness must become engrained and embedded in our minds.** Let your being be immersed in His love and acceptance.

Know, down deep, that you are precious just because God says so, has proven it by the cross, and validated it by the resurrection!

What does this do for you?

1. It sets you **free** to live out the fruit of His Spirit because of "want to" not "have to". (Gal 5:22-23)
2. Fully understanding your worth, you can **freely** show others theirs. (Mt 22:39)
3. When the world batters you with its empty philosophy, you can turn your head, mount up on wings as an eagle, and **rise** above it. (Is 40:28-31)
4. You can uphold yourself with this **biblical fact** when you're tempted to be depressed and discouraged: "God says I'm precious, so I am." (Eph 6:10-18)
5. Since your value is not based on what you do, **you "can do" without fear.** (1 Jn 4:16-18)

Understanding your preciousness is the bottom line, the foundational basis, for all of your life as a fully dedicated follower of Jesus Christ, a disciple.

Lord Jesus, help me to know, deep in my being, how precious I am to You, and as I do, help me to understand how precious others are to You. Please give me Your eyes and Your heart for myself and for everyone else. Thank You, Lord.

Other passages for your prayerful consideration:
Mt 5-7; Jn 2:23-25; 5:41-44; 6:1-15; 13:34-35; 15: 1-12; 17:20-23; Phil 2: 5

Journaling: Write down some of the ways the Lord has shown you how precious you are to Him.

Day Two:
I Am a Partaker of God's Nature.

*His divine power has given us everything we need for life and godliness through our knowledge of Him who called us by His own glory and goodness. Through these He has given us His very great and precious promises, so that through them you might become **partakers** in the divine nature and escape the corruption in the world caused by evil desires. (2 Pt 1:3-4, NIV, NASB)*

One of the greatest compliments I've ever received came written on a Father's Day Card from my son, Richard. He wrote, "When I was at home, I'd wake up, go in the kitchen, and see my dad reading his Bible. Now I'm a man and when I get up, I start my day reading my Bible." I'm glad he didn't "partake" of some of the other "nature" he saw in me!

A few years ago, I was telling Richard about how the ministry concept of Win and Grow was forming in my mind. When I finished, he had only one little bit of advice. *"Dad, just be the branch."* (Jn 15:1-8) It was so simple, yet so profound. **Just be connected to Jesus, and live like you know you are!**

1. You want to know God's will? *Just be the branch.*
2. You want to do God's will? *Just be the branch.*
3. Need victory over temptation? *Just be the branch.*
4. You want to touch another life? *Just be the branch.*

God is imparting His very nature into us! This is an amazing fact!

**His passion, His purposes, His thoughts,
His dreams are becoming ours! Incredible!**

"Delight yourself in the Lord, and He will give you the desires of your heart." (Ps 37:4) Does this mean God will give us whatever we want? Try this interpretation: He will place desires into your heart. **He will make your heart like His.** That may sound crazy, but the Word says you are partaking of His nature.

I can hear you asking, "OK, what do I have to do?" **Flip through Philippians with me:** *. . . He who began a good work in you will carry it on to completion . . . Your attitude should be the same as that of Christ Jesus . . . it is God who works in you to will and to act according to His good purpose . . . that I may gain Christ and be found in Him . . . I can do everything through Him Who gives me strength. . . My God will meet all your needs . . . .* (Phil 1:6, 2:5 & 13, 3:9, 4:13 & 19)

I like the way the King James Version states Phil 2:5. It says, *"Let this mind be in you which was also in Christ Jesus."* Yes, we have to do something. We have to do the **letting** and our Emmanuel, God with us, will do the rest.

26

One last thought: In the center of the word "obey" is "BE". Fully submit your heart to the Lord every day; then just **BE yourself** - just **BE the branch. He will express Himself through you**. (Gal 5:6b; Eph 2:10)

*Father, help me to **just be the branch** allowing You to speak and act through me. Thank You, Lord.*

Other passages for your prayerful consideration:
Mt 28:20b; Jn 14:16-18, 23, 15:1-8, 16:7-15; Gal 5:6b; Heb 13:5b; 1 Jn 4:16-17

Journaling: Make a list of the fruit of the Spirit (Gal 5:22-23) and other aspects of God's nature that come to mind. Think about how He is imparting these qualities into your life and transforming you into the image of His Son, Jesus.

Day Three:
My Passion (Heart) Is God-given.

*A man with leprosy came to Him and begged Him on his knees. "If You are willing, You can make me clean." Filled with **compassion**, Jesus reached out His hand and touched the man. "I am willing," He said, "Be clean!" Immediately the leprosy left him and he was cured.* (Mk 1:40-42)

*Never be lacking in **zeal**, but keep your **spiritual fervor**, serving the Lord.* (Rom 12:11)

" **M**r. K, Mr. K, Maurice died!" My 6th Grade class and I had finished our monthly visit to a convalescent home near the school. I had just gotten out of my car in the parking lot of Taco Bell where we were going to eat lunch, and Brandon, with crew cut, ears sticking out, his red face beaming with a smile, came running up to me. (Yes, running in parking lots was a "no-no.") Somehow this news did not match Brandon's face. Seeing the confusion in my expression, he excitedly explained. "Last month, he asked Jesus into his heart! Maurice is in heaven!" His face was still lit up. This boy had come to my class a very depressed and discouraged student. Early in the year he accepted Jesus as his Savior and Lord, and his outlook quickly began to change! I didn't scold Brandon for running. My heart was full. I just rejoiced with him, and we prayed for Maurice's family.

The Bible uses the word "zeal" to depict passion in a positive way. There are two Greek words translated as "zeal". One is pronounced *spoude* (with a long "e"). It means **earnestness, diligence, eagerness, concern, special urgency, and devotion.** The other is *zelos* (also with a long "e") which adds **ardent** and **deep** to the adjectives describing *spoude*, and also says **having a deep commitment to a Person or cause.** The Thorndike and Barnhart Dictionary (Barnhart, Barnhart, and World Book Inc. 1986) defines "zeal" as **eager desire or effort, earnest enthusiasm, and fervor.** One who is "zealous" is described as being **actively enthusiastic.** It defines "passion" as a very strong emotion and points out that the suffering of Jesus on the cross is called "The Passion."

How did my young disciple, Brandon, get his passion for souls? Someone might graciously say that he picked it up from me. I believe, by God's grace, I was enabled to inspire him and other students, but human inspiration can only go so far. **Worldly ambition is not godly passion.** You can't just work yourself up and kick yourself in the pants. Getting the passion of Jesus requires only one thing from you: praying and asking God for it. **God will not only fill you with His passion for souls; He will sustain the zeal He puts into your heart.** Remember, you are partaking of His nature. I recently found Brandon, my student from the 1980's, on Facebook. When Dona and I had lunch with him and his wife, Thuy, we could easily see that he still has a **God-given passion to win and grow disciples!**

However, when you look within, you may find more complacency than passion. Scripture teaches that in our weakness, God is made strong. (1 Cor 1:18-31) Pray, beginning with confession, and ask for God's help. Acknowledge your weakness. You will find yourself walking in the light with His strength and zeal. He will replace complacency with embers that burn with deep, enthusiastic **compassion** for people.

> *He who believes in Me, as the Scripture has said, out of his heart will*
> *flow rivers of living water.*
> (Jesus in Jn 7:38—NKJ)

Lord, I confess that I'm often complacent about the gospel. Please give me Your passion (heart) for people, and help me to see myself and others the way You do. In my weakness, be strong. Thank You, Father.

Other passages for your prayerful consideration:
Mt 22:36-40; Mk 12:28-31; Lk 4:18-19; Acts 4:19-20; Rom 10:8-17; 2 Cor 5:17-21

Journaling: Write out the people, things, and activities that inspire you and give you energy. Are there passages and stories from the Bible that make your heart burn with excitement when you read them? Which one does so the most?

Day Four:
His Purpose Is My Perspective.

*In Him (Christ), we were also chosen . . . according to the plan of Him Who works out everything in conformity with **the purpose of His will**, in order that we . . . might be for the praise of His glory. . . . His intent was that now, through the Church, the manifold wisdom of God should be made known to the rulers and authorities in the heavenly realms, according to **His eternal purpose**, which He accomplished in Christ Jesus our Lord.*
(Eph 1:11-12, 3:10-11)

"I don't get it! When I try to pray, it's just dark clouds - nothing!" Manuel was frustrated. We'd been trying for days to explain how he could have a new life in Christ.

Finally, my partner gave him an analogy. "Manuel," he explained, "when your little girl is roller-skating on the sidewalk, she's not thinkin' about you, but if she trips and skins her knee, what's the first word out of her mouth? 'Daddy!' That's what we do with God. We roller-skate through life and don't think about Him until we fall down. And how do you respond to your little girl's cry?" Manuel's face began to brighten. My partner assured him, "God responds the same way to us."

With color rising in his cheeks, Manuel cried, "I get it!" He prayed with us and was forever changed! God's perspective had become his!

A different perspective is gained by viewing from another vantage point. **From the perspective of God's purpose we see more clearly.** Before, Manuel could only see his despair, but when he looked from the angle of a father instead of a victim, he saw hope. He found purpose. Perhaps you've read Rick Warren's book, *The PURPOSE DRIVEN Life.*(Warren 2002) In it, Rick answers the question, "What am I here for?" He spends the rest of the book explaining that you and I were made on purpose, for a purpose – one much bigger than you or me; **we are made for God's purpose**!

We see at least three things in the passages from Ephesians (above):

1. We were made "for the praise of His glory."
2. His purpose was "accomplished in Christ Jesus our Lord."
3. This fact is made known "through the Church" (us).

God's purpose is to be in relationship with you and with everyone, so we can *all* live for His glory! In Christ, He made that possible! This is great news! We receive this perspective at salvation, and we spend the rest of our lives growing more like our Savior and Lord.

What did God do to make relationship with us possible? God put skin on. (Jn 1:1-14) Then He said, "Now you, **be Me with skin on**." (Jn 20:21; 1st Jn 4:17-19, paraphrase) *From now on we regard no one from a worldly point of view. . . . If anyone is in Christ, he is a new creation; the old has gone, the new has come! All* *this is from God, Who reconciled us to Himself in Christ and gave us the ministry of reconciliation.* (2 Cor 5:16-18)

> **Here's the center of Perspective and Purpose: God gave us two Great Commandments and one Great Commission that can be summed up: Love God, Love People, Win the Lost, and Grow Disciples.**
> (Mt 22:36-40, 28:18-20, 1 Pt 3:15)

Lord, make Your purpose mine. Help me to see myself and everyone else from a new vantage point, through Your eyes. Deep in my heart, I want to be "Jesus with skin on" for those around me. Thank You, Lord.

Other passages for your prayerful consideration:
Lk 4:18-19; Jn 3:16-17; Rom 12:1-2; Phil 1:6, 2:5. . .12-13; 2 Pt 3:9; 1 Jn 4:7-21

Journaling: Write down The Great Commandments and the Great Commission (references above). Insert your name: _____ , love the Lord your God . . ._____ , all authority . . . Therefore _____ , go . . . . What are your feelings?

Day Five:
Patience Brings God's Peace.

*The Lord. . .is **patient** with you, not wanting anyone to perish, but everyone to come to repentance.* (2 Pt 3:9)

*Love is **patient**. . . .* (1 Cor. 13:4)

*For He Himself is our **peace** . . . .* (Eph 2:14)

"Hurry up! I can't believe we're late again!" It's a typical Sunday morning; we're rushing around and trying to get gone. Four year old Matthew is on the steps of our sunken living room working with great concentration on his laces. "Oh man!" I rush to quickly tie his shoes.

In the middle of my carnality, the Lord spoke to my heart, "One day, you will WISH you could tie this boy's shoes." Wow! I wasn't praying piously; I was not displaying any aspect of the fruit of the Spirit, nor was I personifying Paul's description of love. (Gal 5:16-26, 1 Cor 13:4-8) The Lord literally broke into my self-centered heart in order to teach me something about patience and all the other virtues that go with it.

"Father, You are so holy, righteous, and full of grace. Thank you." I repented. Matthew is a young father himself now, and he's very patient and loving with his two boys. I am so grateful!

It's been said jokingly for years now in Christian circles, "Lord, I need patience, and I need it NOW!" OK, start by being patient with yourself! Slow down, stop, think, and pray. Be honest. Ask yourself how you're doin' with this virtue. Are you quick to beat yourself up with your spiritual stick? Are you ready to pounce on anyone else who does not meet your expectations with the quick rod of self-righteousness? Perhaps you're tough on yourself and everyone else. **For me, it was interesting to reflect on the close relationship between impatience and anger.** Anger: now that was tough to overcome! My lack of patience was rooted in anger, which came out of pride, which was born of fear, the mother of all sin. (1 Jn 4:16-21)

He is patient with you. . . (2 Pt 3:9) . . . **What do I want instead of anxiety? Peace.** *Let the peace of God rule* (like an umpire) *in your hearts. . .* (Col 3:15) Peace is the goal! For me, I had to repent of ungodly anger. (Yes, there is a righteous, self-controlled, anger. Eph 4: 26-27) With a repentant heart, I meditated on every passage in the Bible regarding anger. I developed acts of repentance, strategies, and eventually I had to be **patient with myself**. I began to get a handle on it. I began to know peace.

Know Jesus; Know Peace . . . No Jesus, No Peace

Your situation may be different, but let me share some handles for gaining patience and peace:

1. First, receive God's patience with you. Recognize that He's needed to extend it and that you've needed to receive it. Recall specifics and gratefully receive God's forgiveness all over again. **Fall in love with the fact that God is patient with you.**

2. Anticipate and **practice** (another "P" word): Realize that **you will face challenges to your patience**. Who needs it when everything is going smoothly? When those **opportunities** to display patience come, practice. Take a deep breath, pray; **let the peace of God rule** (like an umpire) in your heart.

3. **Rejoice; repent.** Rejoice in your successes and give thanks to God. Repent when you fail and give thanks to God, for He is patient with you.

Lord, I am a partaker of Your nature, and You are patient. Jesus, You are my peace. Help me to be patient with myself and toward others, and fill me with the peace that can't be taken away. Thank You, Jesus.

Other passages for your prayerful consideration:
Prv 14:29-30, 15:18, 16:32, 19:11; Eccl 7:8-9; Jn 14:27; Rom 12:9-21; Jas 1:19, 5:7-11

Journaling: Make acrostics for the words P-A-T-I-E-N-C-E and P-E-A-C-E. What words come to mind for each letter? Apply them to your goal of more patience and peace.

Day Six:
I Can Meet Obstacles with Perseverance!

Because the Sovereign Lord helps Me, I will not be disgraced. Therefore have I set my face like flint, and I know I will not be put to shame. (Is 50:7)

*As time approached for Him to be taken up to heaven, Jesus **resolutely (steadfastly, steadily with an iron will, gathered up His courage and steeled Himself to, firmly resolved to, steadfastly and determinedly, set His face like flint and)** set out for Jerusalem.* (Lk 9:51, Amplified)

V arsity Football record: 0 – 11! In 1961, I went to the brand new Western High School in Las Vegas, NV, as an 8th grader. There were no seniors. Head football coach, Larry Fromhart, had very little to work with. As I recall, our varsity squad scored just 26 points for the whole year, but Coach Fromhart was not one to give up! In 1962, our team lost the Southern Nevada Conference championship game 14-12. By 1963 we were in the state championship game. Western lost that game to Reno. The next year, our Warriors' state championship streak began and lasted through 1966. No other Southern Nevada AAA football team has won three consecutive state titles. Coach was described as being tough but fair, one who taught great fundamentals and always got the most out of his players. When Coach Fromhart died in 1999, his line coach, Del Foster, said, "He understood the kids real well and the kids respected him." Coach Fromhart knew how to overcome obstacles with perseverance.

Perseverance comes with the eyes of hope, a heart of peace, and a spirit of joy!

Jesus, ". . .for the joy set before Him endured the cross. . ." (Heb 12:2) Isaiah prophesied of our Savior's determination hundreds of years before He came. (Is 52:13-53:12) Early in Luke's gospel he describes the Lord's attitude concerning His mission. (See Lk 9:51 above) There would be many obstacles still to overcome – Gethsemane, the mock trial, the beatings, the cross, the weight of our sin, and the grave. The Father was also determined. He could have called it all off: "Forget it Son; they're not worth it; c'mon home." But **we were worth it!** Our Lord persevered and rose from the grave on the first Easter Sunday morning!

So, here you are. It's your turn. What's your record so far, 0 – 11? Worse? In whose eyes are you measuring your success or failure? **God hangs your drawings on His fridge!** You are the apple of His eye! You are hidden under the shadow of His wings! (Ps 17:8) He never stops thinking about you! (Ps 139:17-18) He Who began a good work in you will complete it in Christ Jesus! Yes, you can do all things through Christ who strengthens you! (Phil 1:6, 4:13)

John's story of the resurrection of Lazarus in chapter 11 contains an important detail for our discussion here. Jesus said, *"Let us go back to Judea."* (vs. 7) *"But Rabbi,"* they said, *"a short while ago the Jews tried to stone You, and yet You are going back there?"* (vs. 8) Jesus had decided to raise Lazarus from the dead, and as they were leaving, Thomas (yes, doubting Thomas – not Peter, not John) said to the rest of the disciples, *"Let us also go, that we may die with Him."* (vs. 16) Thomas later became a missionary to India, and according to the Syriac version of the *Acts of Thomas*, was martyred about the year AD 72.

Every disciple must learn to persevere in God's grace and by His strength.

Lord, as one who is precious to You and a partaker of Your nature, with Your passion, help me to fulfill my purpose in You with perseverance. Tough times will come, but You are Lord at ALL times. Thank You, Father.

Other passages for your prayerful consideration:
Joseph's story - Gn 37, 39-50 (all); David's story - 1 Sm 16 (all)—2 Sm 5; the books of Ezra/Nehemiah; Gal 6:9; Heb 11-12:13; 2 Pt 1:3-11

Journaling: Don Sarver, a longtime friend, once shared about a trial. He closed with this statement: "I'm just glad He thought enough of me to allow me to go through it." Recall and write down how God brought you through a trial. Are you facing one now? Ask the Lord to bring you through it in a way that honors Him.

Day Seven:
Précis: I Can Practice the Presence of God.

*I am the Vine (Source); you are the branches. If a person remains in Me and I in him, he will bear much fruit; **apart from Me you can do nothing**.* (Jn 15:5)

P récis: a concise (precise) or abridged statement – OK, let me try it: "Because you are **precious** to God and a **partaker** of His nature, you have His **passion** and **perspective** to fulfill His **purpose** with **patience, peace,** and **perseverance**." Not a short enough précis? How about the lesson from my son, Richard?

"Dad, just be the branch." (Day 2)

Imagine that you're one of the original 12 disciples (anyone except Judas). You're hangin' out with Jesus. You have supper together. He washes your feet. He says a bunch of really confusing and hard to hear stuff like, "*. . .it is for your good that I am going away.. . .*" (Jn 16:7) If I'm there, I'm thinking, "What? You're the Guy! You heal the sick, cast out demons, give sight to the blind, make the lame walk, feed thousands with a boy's lunch, raise the dead, and teach like no one ever has before and never will again! It's for my **'good'** that You're going away?" Fortunately for us Jesus didn't reply with a simple, "Yep."

Put yourself in another Bible scene: You're in a boat on the Sea of Galilee, and a violent storm comes up. It's so bad, you're afraid you're going to die! Jesus is asleep. You go get Him. "Wake up Lord, we're gonna drown!" You know the rest of the story in Matthew, chapter 8. How about the sea story in Matthew 14? You're in the boat with the other disciples, and the wind's comin' up again. Suddenly, it's not the wind that's freaking you out. Somebody is coming toward you, walking on the water! You figure out that it's Jesus after Peter gets out of the boat and starts walking towards the Lord on the water. They get into the boat and the only thing that dies is the wind. While on earth, Jesus could be apart from the disciples, but they would never be separated from the Holy Spirit. "*it is for your **good** that I am going away. . .*" (Jn 16:7) "*. . .Unless I go away, the Counselor will not come to you. . .*" (Jn 16:7) On Pentecost, 10 days after Jesus went into heaven and 50 days after the resurrection, they began to understand. (Acts 1:8, 2:1-47)

Suffer through Dave's Version for a moment: "I can be separated from you, Friends, because I'm flesh and blood, but the Counselor, the Advocate, the Comforter; the Holy Spirit will always be there. Through Him, I and My Father, will be with you and in you 24/7!" *He* (the Holy Spirit) *is* <u>with you</u> *and will be* <u>in you</u>. . . .*If anyone loves Me, he will obey My teaching. My Father will love him, and* <u>we will come to him and make our home with him</u>. (Jn 14:17, 23) **The Holy Trinity lives in your heart!** What did Jesus say at the end of the Great Commission in Matthew 28? "*And surely I am with you* <u>always</u>, *even to the end of the age.*" (vs. 20) He knew His charge to us would be hard, so He reassured us. It's like He was saying, "You can do this because I'm going to help you!"

Practice the **Presence** of God! As you go through the rest of this devotional/study guide, you're going to discover more about how God made you and equipped you to obey the Great Commandments and fulfill the Great Commission. There will be tools that you can use with your own God-given personality, passion, and gifts. **Remain open to the Spirit**. Let's see what God does!

Jesus, help me to walk in the awareness of Your presence in me. Thank You, Lord.

Other passages for your prayerful consideration:
Jn 13-17; Rom 8 (all); 2 Cor 4 & 5 (all); Gal 5:16-25; Eph 2:1-10; Phil 1:6, 2:5-13, 3:7-11, 4:4-8, 13,19; Col 3:1-17; Heb 4: 11-16; Jas 3:13-18; 1 Jn 1:5-2:2, 4:4, 13-21; Rv 2:7, 11, 17, 29, 3:6, 13, 22 (Read the context and make personal applications.)

Journaling: When do you sense God's presence the most? . . . The least? What can you do to become more aware that Jesus is always with you?

Week 2

How Has God Made Me?

Day Eight:
What Are My Spiritual Gifts?

Follow the way of love and eagerly desire spiritual gifts. . . . .
(1 Cor 14:1)

"No, not yet, Daddy! Not yet."
"Sweetheart, I have to let go sometime."
"Not yet, Daddy."
"But Honey, I can't run anymore! I have to let go!"

With wheels wobbling, Jenny headed down the sidewalk. Crash! She got up and looked back at her dad. She had gotten farther than the last time. She shrugged off a small scratch. A broad smile broke onto her face. She was going to do this! Her dad had bought her this bike for a birthday gift, and she was determined to ride it. So, Dad took hold of the seat again and down the sidewalk he ran. This time, there were no pleas not to let go, and when he did, Jenny was steadier. She was off! Oh how she loved the wind in her face! She'd done it! Her new bicycle was a very special gift! She so enjoyed learning to use it and got better and better at it!

Like Jenny's father, **our heavenly Father has given us gifts and wants to help us learn to use them**. What do you know about spiritual gifts? Perhaps you've taken an assessment. Are you using your spiritual gifts? Are there gifts that you'd like to use more effectively? **Have you thought about how your spiritual gifts can help you obey the Great Commandments to love God and people and to be personally active in the fulfillment of the Great Commission by sharing the gospel and making disciples?** (Mt 22:36-40, 28:18-20) These passages are the focal point of the Christian life.

What about the "tongues" thing? That's scary! Let's quickly deal with it – first, the extremes. On one end of the spectrum - "If you speak in tongues you are demon-possessed." WHERE DOES THE BIBLE TEACH THAT?!? On the other end - "If you don't speak in tongues you're not saved." WHERE DO THE SCRIPTURES SAY THAT?!? So, what is this gift? It is simply speaking in a language that one has not learned but is granted through the Holy Spirit. This language can be used privately for personal edification. (1 Cor 14:4, 14-15) Or, it can be used in the public worship service where it must be interpreted. (1 Cor 4:13) Paul deals with this gift very clearly in 1 Cor 14. Read the whole chapter, along with chapters 12 and 13. Twelve and fourteen have been described as two good pieces of whole grain bread, and chapter 13 (the "love chapter") is the meat, cheese, tomatoes, lettuce, avocado, mayo, and. . . .

To some, the whole subject of spiritual gifts is a little scary. For example, we say we believe in miracles, but when we're asked to pray for one or need a miracle ourselves, well, that's different! The working of miracles is simply another one of the spiritual gifts. **The Bible says that everyone in the Body of Christ has spiritual gifts working through them, and the Bible gives instructions about their use.** *There are different kinds of gifts, but the same Spirit. There are different kinds of service, but the same Lord. There are different kinds of working, but the same God works all of them in all men.* (1 Cor 12:4-6)

Spiritual gift surveys are put together mainly from three places in scripture: Rom 12:1-8, 1 Cor 12 (to be read in context with chapters 13 and 14), and Eph 4:11-16. Your church may have one or **you can go on line at www.churchgrowth.org and take one free of charge.** There is also a spiritual gifts survey in Appendix B. Your homework is to take a spiritual gifts survey.

Lord, help me to be tuned to Your Holy Spirit, to discover my spiritual gifts and to understand how to use them to further Your kingdom. Thank You, Jesus.

Other passages for your prayerful consideration:
Ps 139:13-14; Mt 7:7-12; Lk 11:11-13; 1 Cor 1:7; Eph 4: 7-8; Heb 2:1-4; 1 Pt 4:7-11

Journaling: Write down 2 – 5 of your highest scoring spiritual gifts. How is God using those gifts? Are there other ways they can be used? What gifts would you like to develop more? How might the Holy Spirit open doors for you through your gifts to share your faith verbally?

Day Nine:
What Are My Personality Strengths?

*For by the grace given me I say to every one of you: Do not think of yourself more highly (or more lowly) than you ought, but rather **think of yourself with sober judgment**, in accordance with the measure of faith God has given you.* (Rom 12:3)

I watched from a little distance as Dona told the "Wide Mouthed Frog" joke to a small circle of friends. Every time the "wide mouthed frog" spoke, she opened her mouth as wide as she could, which made the story very funny. In the story, the frog goes from animal to animal asking, "What do you like to eat?" To each reply, the frog answers, "Oh, that's nice." Dona's mouth is literally gaping until she gets to the alligator who answers, "I eat wide-mouthed frogs." Dona made her mouth as tiny as she could: "Oh, that's nice." I thought, "There's a girl who doesn't worry about her appearance so much that she can't distort her face to tell a cute joke." That's when our story began. I was falling in love with her and 39 years later, as I write, my Precious is still patiently working to try to make a prince out of a frog! "Lord, help her!"

Why tell that story on a page about personality? Simple – Dona had learned to accept herself the way God made her. **We need to know our strengths and weaknesses so we can cooperate with the Spirit as He transforms us into the image of Christ.** To help you get a starting place, you need to take a personality assessment. I know this might make you feel a little uncomfortable. I did, but I learned a lot about myself. "What if I find something I don't like? I know I probably will, and I don't want to!" Set those worries aside. Hey, there's no guilt or condemnation in Jesus. (Rom 8:1-2) Go back to **Day One: You are Precious!** God says so; don't argue with Him! **A personality assessment just gives us knowledge.** It helps us to walk in the light. (1 Jn 1:5-2:2) It's a tool to help us *"think of ourselves with sober judgment."* (above) Then, we just re-submit ourselves to God. You may have taken an assessment. I've taken many. Perhaps you're familiar with some of these one-word descriptions of the four basic personality types:

Orientation	Personality Types			
Project	Choleric*	D*	Lion*	The Captain*
People	Sanguine*	I*	Otter*	The Social Director*
People	Melancholic**	S**	Golden Retriever**	The Steward**
Project	Phlegmatic**	C**	Beaver **	The Navigator**
	* tend to be extroverts; ** tend to be introverts			

I've seen other designations and I'm sure you have too. I like Dr. John Trent's (StrongFamilies.com) approach because he doesn't see people as being "stuck in a box." He believes and teaches that we can achieve balance by using our strengths to overcome our weaknesses. Jesus was perfectly balanced. **What we all want is Christ-likeness.** In Appendix C, you will find the Dr. Trent's LOGB® personality assessment. You can also find free personality inventories on line. We all have Ps 139: 23-24 as our prayer: *"Search me, O God, and know my heart; test me and know my anxious thoughts. See if there is any offensive way in me, and lead me in the way everlasting."* And we have this assurance: . . .*He Who began a good work in you will be faithful to complete it.* (Phil 1:6) So again, you have homework. Take a personality assessment. Don't worry. It'll be fun!

Lord, You made me; help me to know myself. Teach me to serve You and Your kingdom. May I work towards its increase as I grow with the gifts and personality You gave me. Thank You, Jesus.

Other passages for your prayerful consideration:
Ps 139; 1 Jn 3:1-3, 4:17-19; 2 Cor 3:17-18; 2 Pt 1:3-11

Journaling: When you looked at your assessment, did you think, "Yep, that's me?" Or, were you surprised? How can you use your strengths to help you in areas where you want to grow?

Day Ten:
Godly Character Trumps Weaknesses.

Therefore, since we have been justified through faith, we have peace with God through our Lord Jesus Christ. . .and we rejoice in the hope of the glory of God. . .we rejoice in our sufferings, because we know that suffering produces perseverance; perseverance, character; and character, hope. And hope does not disappoint us, because God has poured out His love into our hearts by the Holy Spirit,. . . .
(Rom 5:1-5)

I 'm in my wife's arms apologizing for some kind of self-centered behavior. It's a very serious moment. She chuckles! I get upset – "What!?" (How quickly non-Christ-like attitudes can resurge!)

"Well, I've been praying about that," she replies simply. I smile. Dona had not said a word to me about this personality flaw, but she had spoken to our Father about it; then *He* spoke to me.

Two questions:

1. How can we make positive changes to our personality "flaws"?
2. How can we develop spiritual gifts that we don't have or that are low on the gift assessment?

First, we need to know that those "flaws" are the flip side of strengths. Secondly, and more importantly, **God has put a desire into each of us to want to be like His Son.** This devotional and study guide assumes that you are a fully devoted follower of Jesus Christ – a disciple. All Christians are in different places in their development, but we all have a God-given desire to be Christ-like. Perhaps you recall the story told in Luke 9, beginning at verse 51: Jesus and His disciples are on their way to a Samaritan village and they receive word that they're not welcome. *When the disciples, James and John saw this, they asked, "Lord, do You want us to call fire down from heaven and destroy them!"* (vs. 54) "No, 'Sons of Thunder' we'll just go on to the next village." (Mk 3:17 – my version) James was the first apostle to be martyred, and John came to be known as The Apostle of Love. **Our flaws are being transformed.** Here's a word of caution regarding strengths: If not submitted to the Lordship of Jesus, they can become weaknesses, maybe even without us realizing it! Stay humble.

John's transformation came about the same way yours and mine does. He "let" the attitude of Jesus become his. (Phil 2:5-KJV) He let the Holy Spirit transform his mind. (Rom 12:1-2) He was a partaker of God's nature. (2 Pt 1:3-11) He was connected to the Vine. (Jn 15:1-8) *"Dad, just be the branch."* (Richard Kachele – Day 2)

Godly Character Trumps Personality Flaws
and Weakness in the Area of Spiritual Gifts

Now that you've taken the spiritual gift and personality assessments, you've got a handle for your prayers. Without guilt, knowing that your value is beyond measure, simply lift yourself to your heavenly Father.

Let me share a personal testimony. One of the personality assessments that I took had defining words for each of the four basic types. I scored so low on the "fun-loving" scale that the word used to describe me was "suspicious"! By nature, I am not an "Otter!" When I saw that, I prayed, "Lord, help me!" Then, I pushed myself. I posted one word reminders hidden all over my classroom – "SMILE." I went to gatherings (Dona loves them.). I joked; I laughed. I learned to laugh at myself. You know what? I've improved. I've made progress in the "other people orientation" area (Golden Retriever) too. God did it! I should say, "God's doing it." Like you, I'm a work in progress.

God, I submit to You in the development of my character. Fill my weakness with Your strength. Do the same type of conversion in me that You did in John the Disciple. Thank You for being so patient.

Other passages for your prayerful consideration:
Phil 1:6, 2:5. . .12-13; 2 Pt 3:9; 1 Jn 4:7-21

Journaling: List the Godly character traits that God is forming in you. How can God's character, being formed in you, help to overcome perceived flaws and weakness? Remember, we all fall short and into the arms of grace. As you think about this, don't allow any guilt or condemnation creep in. (Rom 8:1-2) Stay positive.

Day Eleven:
I Am Discovering God's Passion in Me.

Even zeal is not good without knowledge . . . (Prv 19:10)

Remember the story about the little girl that got a new bike for a gift? (Day 8) She had seen bigger kids riding their bikes. Passion was born when she saw them having fun. It was kindled when she heard them laughing, watching the wind blow their hair back. Passion grew. She wanted a bike. The passion was still there even after crashes. Her courage and confidence continued to grow. She got better at it. She became addicted to the feeling of freedom as she flew down the sidewalk! She still occasionally crashed but always got up again. She learned to **use the gift** that was **born of passion. Passion is the mother of gifting.**

"Dad, the fire's goin' out."

"Brrrr, yeah, it's gettin' cold, eh Son? Look at all those stars!"

"You gonna let it die?" He didn't need to worry. It was his first camp out, but his dad had done it many times. He knew how to take care of a fire. "Get a little closer." Happy to follow this direction, the boy edged nearer to the embers. Dad threw some twigs on them. Nothing happened. "Get your head down low and blow on those ashes just a little." Nothing. "Blow a little harder." Flame! The fire suddenly came to life. The boy jerked back. "Reach over and get three or four small logs and lay 'em on top." More flame! "Now, get that big one." The boy set the largest log he could pick up on top. He could feel the much welcomed heat. Just the same, he snuggled up into his dad's lap, warm and content.

Like a campfire, **passion can be kindled and rekindled** even when it seems the fire has gone completely out. You poke the coals, blow on them a little, and throw on another log. **Like the dad in the story above, your heavenly Father will hold you and teach you about "fire."** What is the passion of His heart? Is it not that everyone will enter into and grow in relationship with Him? Are we not partakers of His nature? (2 Pt 1:3-8) Aren't we being transformed into His likeness? (2 Cor 3:17-18) Jesus has a passion for souls! **Your God-given passion will give life to your gifting!**

Do you ever pray for friends or relatives who are not walking with Jesus? **You have coals burning within your heart.** Do you ever think "I wonder if they know Jesus?" as you pass by people, check out at the store, or are waited on at a restaurant? **You have God's passion for souls!** Do you support missions work? **You're participating indirectly in the fulfillment of the Great Commission** (winning souls and growing disciples). Do songs about the cross and those that we sing during missions emphasis week stir your heart? **You are growing in obedience to the Great Commandments** (to love God and people). Is there a better way to obey them than to see the Great Commission fulfilled? You may crash a time or two but you can learn and grow in your ability to share the gospel and help someone grow into maturity. **The more you ride your bicycle, the more confident and fruitful you will become.** (Day 8)

Lord, You are passionate about being in relationship with people. I am too, but I confess that I have more fear than fire. May I receive more of Your passion? Teach me to use my gifts, with my personality, to love people into Your kingdom and help them to grow. Thank You, Father.

Other passages for your prayerful consideration:
Mt 4:18-20 and 26:69-75; Acts 4:8-31; Acts 9:1-31; Eph 5:15-18; 1 Thes 5:16-24

Journaling: Your **S**piritual **G**ifts, Personality, **P**assions (**H**eart), **A**bilities, and **E**xperiences reveal your **SHAPE.(Rees 2006)** Use the acronym below to think about how God has made you.

Spiritual Gifts
Heart (Passion)
Abilities
Personality
Experiences

Day Twelve:
I Can Embrace My Giftedness and Fulfill God's Purpose!

. . .Whatever you do, do it all for the glory of God. (1 Cor 10:31)

Do you recall the Swedish chef on the Muppet Show? He taught us how to make a chocolate mousse: "First you get the chocolate. Then you find the moose. . .Here Moosey, Moosey. . . børk. . ." (Google him for some hilarious You Tube video.) **How do you put all that you've gathered into the recipe that is you, and how can God use you to fulfill His purpose**? That's a question we'll focus on today and the next two days.

Of course, you know that the Lord will never be finished with you until you are with Him. Think of Abraham. He and Sarah had Isaac when he was 100 years old. He had believed God and it was credited to him as righteousness. He had lived for the Lord for decades. *Then God said, "Take your son, Isaac, whom you love, and go to the region of Moriah. Sacrifice him there as a burnt offering on one of the mountains I will tell you about."* (Gn 22:2) God was still not finished with Abraham! Is He finished with you . . . with me? No way! He loves us too much.

This story has a powerful application for us. How could Abraham obey God without question? How could Isaac, by then a young man, allow himself to be placed on that pile of wood? Now, fill in the blank: "How can I _____? **The answer to all our questions is found in Hebrews 11:** *By faith. . .* Abraham did what Jesus did; he emptied himself and placed his life completely in the hands of His heavenly Father. (Phil 2:5-11)

How can we characterize faith? First, it's the gift of God. (Eph 2:8-10) It justifies. (Gal 2:16) It is one aspect of the fruit of the Spirit. (Gal 5:22-23) It grows. (2 Cor 10:15) It can be added to. (2 Pt 1:3-11) Faith is the shield that quenches the fiery darts of the enemy. (Eph 6:16) It is evidenced by deeds. (Jas 2:18) Faith is the victory that overcomes the world. (1 Jn 5:1-5) It is that by which the righteous live! (Rom 1:17). *. . .The only thing that counts is faith expressing itself through love.* (Gal 5:6b) I pay attention when the Bible says, *"the only thing that counts."*

Do you remember the story of Eustace in the C.S. Lewis classic, *The Voyage of the Dawn Treader?*(Lewis) It's my favorite story in those wonderful books. If you've read it, you recall that useless Eustace was a boy who turned into a dragon and back to a boy again. Eustace told his story to his friends after being restored to boyhood. He had tried and tried to peel off the dragon skin only to find another layer underneath.

In the story, the Lion (Aslan, a type of Christ) said, "You will have to let Me undress you."

Eustace said, "I was afraid of His claws, I can tell you, but I was pretty nearly desperate now. So I just lay flat on my back and let Him do it. The first tear he made was so deep that I thought it had gone right into my heart. . . . He peeled the stuff right off. . . . He caught hold of me. . .and threw me into the water. . . . After a bit the Lion took me out and dressed me. . .in new clothes." (Read Chapters 6 & 7)

In Lewis' next book in the series, *The Silver Chair*, Eustace was no longer useless; he was the hero!

Like Abraham and like Eustace, **we have to put ourselves completely in the Master's hands.** All of your weaknesses and strengths, your gifts and the lack of them, your personality, and your passion, abilities, and experiences must be placed on the altar. Submit (or re-submit) fully to the love and lordship of Jesus Christ.

Lord, here am I, send me. Thank You for Your call.

Other passages for your prayerful consideration: Phil 4:13

Journaling: How did you fill in the blank? Write an answer for this question: "How can I, with my gifts, personality, passion, ability, and experience, get a sharper focus on obedience to the Great Commandments and the Great Commission?"

Day Thirteen:
I Can Embrace My Personality and Fulfill God's Purpose!

> *. . .Let us throw off everything that hinders. . .and let us run with perseverance the race marked out for us. Let us fix our eyes on Jesus. . .so that we will not grow weary and lose heart.* (Heb 12:1-3)

Okay, time to focus: Have you heard of the 5 "Ws" + an "H"? Good reporters use them in news stories.

1 Who? We are fully devoted followers of Jesus Christ. (1 Pt 3:15a)

2 What? We are committed to obeying the Great Commandments to love God and love people and to do our part to fulfill the Great Commission by winning the lost and growing disciples. (Mt 22:36-40, 28:18-20)

3 Where? *. . .And you will be my witnesses in Jerusalem, and in all Judea and Samaria, and to the ends of the earth.* (Acts 1:8) Let's start with our Jerusalem – our circles of influence. (1 Pt 3:15b)

4 Why? *. . .And how can they hear without someone telling them?* (Rom 10:14)

5 When? *Now is the day of salvation.* (2 Cor 6:2)

H How? *May the God of peace, . . .equip you with everything good for doing His will, and may He work in us what is pleasing to Him, through Jesus Christ. . . . Amen.* (Heb 13:20-21; 1 Pt 3:15c)

You are armed with knowledge about your preciousness and connectedness to Jesus and how God has made you: your spiritual gifts, heart (passion), abilities, personality, and experiences. These provide the telescope and the microscope through which you focus on the **centrality of our faith: loving God, loving people, and making disciples**. Don't worry about what you don't have or feel that you can't do. Begin with how God has made you. He wouldn't tell you to do something that you can't do with His help.

Now, I have a confession to make: I am an evangelist (although it is not my most dominant gift). However, I have learned that to be effective, I need the gift of mercy (in which I scored very low when I took the gift assessment) and all the "service" gifts. Why? It's because the Gospel must be proclaimed in word **and** deed. I can't just *tell* someone about the love of God; I must **demonstrate** His love also. **My passion to see people come to know the Lord drives me to do something unnatural for me – extend mercy and kindness.** I'm learning by watching people with these gifts. Acts of kindness open the door to sharing with words.

Let's turn things around. You may have the gift of mercy but talking to someone about Jesus scares you to death! You can demonstrate the Gospel easily, but proclaiming is not your thing. Yet, **you have a strong desire (passion) to see those whom you love come to know Christ.** What do you do? The theme verse for Win and Grow is 1 Pt 3:15: *In your heart set apart Christ as Lord. Always be prepared to give everyone who asks you to give the reason for the hope that you have. Do this with gentleness and respect.* Think about each sentence in the passage separately. You can lift some to Christ in prayer. You can mark a few passages of scripture in your pocket/purse New Testament or the Bible in your phone. When God opens the door you can tell your story of faith. You can invite a friend to church or a home group. People with other gifts can learn from the evangelist, too.

If you took the spiritual gifts inventory found at www.churchgrowth.org, you saw some stats in the analysis at the end. As the number of users grows, the stats stay pretty constant. Only about 3½% of laity and about 5¼% of clergy have evangelism as their dominant gift. However, I know that **a much larger percentage of us have passion to see the Great Commission fulfilled.** The call of Win and Grow Ministries and the purpose of this devotional/study guide are to nurture passion – to inspire, encourage, and equip <u>*all*</u> of us. Perhaps even the evangelists can learn something and become more effective, too.

Lord, my life is in Your hands. I want to do Your will. Thanks for putting Your heart for people in me.

Other passages for your prayerful consideration: 2 Cor 5:11-21

Journaling: Is there a gap between your passion for people and your personal, active involvement in winning and growing disciples? How can you work with the Holy Spirit to bridge that gap?

Day Fourteen:
With My Passion I Can Fulfill God's Purpose!

In all my prayers for all of you, I always pray with joy because of your partnership in the gospel from day one until now, being confident of this, that He Who began a good work in you will carry it out to completion until the day of Christ Jesus. . . .I can do everything (and anything) through Him Who gives me strength. (Phil 1:4-6, 4:13)

It was amazing how many gang members had shown up to hear David Wilkerson preach his heart out! Even more incredible was the response when he gave the altar call. I was also impressed by the young people who served as altar workers. They were from a new group called "Youth with a Mission" led by an easy-going young man named Loren Cunningham. I'd heard that YWAM's next ministry assignment was a two-week crusade in *Westminster, CA.* I asked if I could join them. I was only sixteen at the time. Loren visited our little church to share his vision one Wednesday night. At one point in his message, he pointed right at me and said, **"The gospel can be shared by anyone, even a kid in a red T-shirt."** I was not yet a fully committed follower of Jesus Christ, but that's another story.

You've seen the passage above pop up before in this devotional/study guide. That's because it's absolutely essential to understanding this reality: God's not looking for you and me; **He's looking for Jesus in you and me** – YOU and ME with our own gifts, personality, and passion. It's not about ability; rather, it's about availability!

The call of Jesus is ours: *The Spirit of the Lord in on Me, because He has anointed Me to preach good news to the poor. He has sent Me to proclaim freedom for the prisoners and recovery of sight for the blind, to release the oppressed, and proclaim the year of the Lord's favor.* (Lu. 4:18-19) Why is this also our call? We're connected to the Vine. (Jn 15:1-8) Remember what Peter and John said when commanded by the Sanhedrin not to preach Jesus? *"We cannot help speaking about what we have seen and heard."* (Acts 4:20)

Growing disciples is the heart (passion) of Jesus.

You are partaking of His nature.

You are becoming more like Him every day.

But you do not need to become someone else! **You can personally and actively participate in the fulfillment of the Great Commission just as you are and just as you are becoming.** Check out 2 Peter 1:3-11 again. (It was the focus of Day 2.) Believers who are **growing** like you and me can be effective and productive! None of us has "arrived." *Not that I have attained all this, or have already been made perfect, but I press on to take hold of that for which Christ Jesus took hold of me.* (Phil 3:12)

Next week, you will focus on your own "Jesus Story." The following weeks of this devotional have to do with equipping. So, let's do what the Billy Graham altar call song says, "Just as I am without one plea. . .I come."

Lord, I come, incomplete in myself, but complete in You. Please keep me inspired and encouraged, sharing Your love in word and in deed. Equip me to be Your hands, Your feet, and Your voice for the people in my circles of influence that You love so much. Thank You, Jesus.

Other passages for your prayerful consideration:
Mt 5:13-16; Jn 4:35-38; Eph 3:11; 1 Pt 2:9

Journaling: Review your own journaling for the first 13 days. Is there anything hindering you from saying, "Here am I Lord, send me."? (Is 6:8) Write those things down and lift them up to the Lord. What do you hope He will do in you over the next five weeks? Will you let Him do it?

Week 3

The Story of My Own Spiritual Journey

Day Fifteen:
When Was I First Aware that I Had a Relationship with Jesus?

The Lord said to Abram, "Leave your country, your people, and your father's household and go to the land I will show you." (Gn 12:1)

♫ I love to tell the story of unseen things above, of Jesus and His glory, of Jesus and His love.

I love to tell the story, because I know 'tis true; it satisfies my longings as nothing else can do.

I love to tell the story, 'twill be my theme in glory, to tell the old, old story of Jesus and His love.

I love to tell the story; more wonderful it seems than all the golden fancies of all our golden dreams.

I love to tell the story, it did so much for me; and that is just the reason I tell it now to thee.

I love to tell the story, 'twill be my theme in glory, to tell the old, old story of Jesus and His love.

I love to tell the story; 'tis pleasant to repeat what seems, each time I tell it, more wonderfully sweet.

I love to tell the story, for some have never heard the message of salvation from God's holy Word.

I love to tell the story, 'twill be my theme in glory, to tell the old, old story of Jesus and His love. ♫

(Hankey 1866)

Some of you have been singing. Some are saying, "What the. . .?" If you're in the second group, may I encourage you to spend some devotional time with a church hymnal? You will be blessed! **We all love a good story. Have you ever told your Jesus Story?** Following Peter's encouragement in 1 Peter 3:15, you will want to learn to tell it in just a few minutes. The purpose of this week's devotions is to help you think about, enjoy, and be able to tell your story to anyone who asks about the hope that you have in your Lord.

"You can't help someone find water until you've first been to the well." (Anonymous) **You'll be blessed as you tell your own story and see how easily**

it naturally combines with His. Understanding your own path to Jesus and your journey with Him will assist you in helping others to discover where they are on theirs.

"My story is so dull! I grew up in church. I can't even remember when I first began to love Jesus and want to serve Him." Wow! That's an amazing story! I wish it were mine! Don't get me wrong – I love the dramatic stories, which leads me to the next objection: "My story is embarrassing to tell." I can relate. I once had a dream (nightmare really) of being a marijuana plantation owner in South America! (That is not easy to say!) Later, as a principal of a Christian school, I was led to tell my story in a chapel. Afterwards, one of the teachers came up to me and said, "Wow Dave, you used to want to be a marijuana plantation owner, and now you run a plantation where we grow kids!" I had never thought of that. "Lord, look what you did." **We *all* have an amazing Jesus story because He is amazing!**

God will lead you to people who <u>NEED</u> to hear <u>YOUR</u> story.

Lord, You've touched my life and caused me to know, love, and want to follow You. You've blessed my life with Your ever presence. Help me to bless another with my Jesus story. Thank You, Lord.

Other passages for your prayerful consideration:
Mt 10:19-20, 12:33-35; Jn 3:1-21, 7:45-52, 19:38-42; Jn 4:4-42; Jn 9:1-41; Acts 9:19, 26:1-32, 10:1-48, 16:22-34; 2 Tm 1:1-7

Journaling: Be blessed in your journaling this week as you contemplate and write out the story of how you came to know Christ, how He's working in your life now, and what you hope He will do with you in the future. Don't worry about the length, etc. You can fine tune it later.

Day Sixteen:
How Has He Guided My Life?

. . .When He, the Spirit of Truth, comes, He will guide you into all truth. (Jn 16: 13)

♫ I can hear my Savior calling,
I can hear my Savior calling,
I can hear my Savior calling,
"Take thy cross and follow, follow me."
Where He leads me I will follow,
Where He leads me I will follow,
Where He leads me I will follow,
I'll go with Him, with Him, all the way. ♫
(Blandy 1890)

Though I was raised by a Christian mom and grandmother, I didn't come to know Jesus personally until I was a young adult. He touched my life when I was bankrupt not just financially, but emotionally, morally, physically, and spiritually. I had a young son at the time, and one of my first prayers was, "Lord, please save Jeff's mother, or find me a Christian wife." About a year and a half later, Dona and I were married. That was nearly 40 years ago. The Lord has allowed us to share this story many times since then. It's fun to tell. Here, I'll simply say that we were both fully committed to Christ. We prayed for His leading and He guided us in **four ways that will serve anyone wanting God's will in his or her life:**

1. We had the witness from the Word of God from our individual daily time with Jesus.
2. We had the witness in our own spirits during daily prayer and meditation.
3. We had the witness of other believers as we sought wise counsel.
4. We had the witness of our circumstances – it worked out!

How has God led your life? What decisions has He helped you to make? When have you strayed from the path and He led you back onto the right road? What has He taught you along the way? What part has the Word of God had in the leading of your life? What part did others play in the way God spoke to you? The answers to these questions will bless you as you contemplate them, and bless anyone God leads you to tell. Notice that I said, ". . .anyone God leads you to tell." This is not about "make it happen" evangelism. That has its place, but **"let it happen" sharing can be very fruitful, especially in a one-on-one situation.** (Day 26)

Yesterday's devotion was about telling your "knowing Jesus is my Savior" story. We need to know it; we need to be ready to tell it. But we also need to remember and tell what God has done since submitting to Him as Lord. **He led you to Himself; He's led you ever since. These stories are part of your being. At the right Holy**

Spirit-led time, they will flow naturally, and therefore, convincingly. You are not in a religion; you're in a relationship with the living God! Try to put yourself in the shoes of someone who doesn't know a God like that! Your story is incredible because Jesus is incredible! You didn't get to where you are by accident. You may be in very difficult circumstances. A pastor acquaintance of mine once shared about his journey with his wife who had cancer. It was a very hard time. He shared how God led and ministered to them. He concluded saying, "We learned not to ask, 'Why, Lord?' but 'What now?'" I recall hearing many stories that have stuck with me. They have encouraged me many times. In the same way, **your life with God will encourage, teach, and help guide others to the abundant life Jesus offers.**

Father, as I think about how You've led me, I'm so grateful for Your faithfulness. Help me to tell others how You have worked in my life. Thank You, Jesus.

Other passages for your prayerful consideration:
Genesis, All of Chapters 24, 37, & 39-45; Ps 78 (all, esp. 14, 53

Journaling: Write down a testimony or two describing how God led and helped you at particular times in the past. These stories may be exactly the ones someone else needs to hear for the encouragement of their faith.

Day Seventeen:
What's God Doing with Me Right Now?

Your word is a lamp to my feet and a light for my path. (Ps 119:105)

Thirty years is a long time. God had blessed and used me in Christian schools, but at the end of the 2009 school year, the one where I was teaching closed its doors. I didn't ask, "Why Lord?" I asked, "What now?" "Do I try to break into a new school as a teacher or principal?" I'd done both. "Do I take my gift to public schools where Christian teachers are on the front lines every day?" None of these options felt right. I continued praying. "OTOEM" (pronounced 'autumn'): "One To One Evangelism Ministries" came to mind. "OTOEM" had been a long time dream. I'd spent my whole Christian life making disciples and teaching others to do the same. "Lord, what are You saying?"

"It's time to follow that dream," was His reply.

Little by little, "OTOEM" grew into "Win and Grow," and *THE RELUCTANT EVANGELIST: Embrace Your Gifts and Fulfill God's Purpose* became the tool the ministry would use to encourage His Body.

What's God doing with me right now? He's helping me to develop this ministry. He's teaching me patience because it's taking a lot of time. He has me reading, studying, praying, and seeking counsel. He's helping me to develop a website: winandgrow. com and to write, get input, edit, and rewrite *THE RELUCTANT EVANGELIST: Embrace Your Gifts and Fulfill God's Purpose*. He's leading day by day in many other ways. While working on Win and Grow, my life hasn't stopped. My wife and I are active in our church and community. We're leading Bible studies. We're sharing our faith and mentoring others. We have children and grandchildren. I work at home and take care of most of the household chores while my wife works at Azusa Pacific University (APU). In all of this I am seeking the Holy Spirit for daily guidance, trying to listen and obey.

Every relationship has a beginning. I love the story of how Dona and I began our journey together. Every relationship has history. We have many wonderful memories collected over the last 39 years. Every relationship has a present. After all these years, I still can't wait to be with my wife after work TODAY!

How your relationship with God began is crucial. Your history with Jesus is very important. The circumstances and situations He's helped you through have brought you to where you are today. **What God is doing in your life currently is a vital part of your ongoing story.** What is the Lord doing with you right now? How is He leading you? What have you learned from the Spirit this week? What sources is He using to speak into your life? What encouragement did you receive from reading the Word this morning? **You serve a living God; He's leading you today, and that's exciting!** How is He helping you to minister to others?

Part of my prayer every day is, "Lord, make me aware of Your presence as I go through my day." **Your story is never-ending because you're in relationship with a living, eternal God who loves and guides you every day, just as He promised.**

This is essential, because you don't know when He will open the door for you to share your story or which part of it will fit the need of the moment. So, think about the past and be aware of the present. God will use what He has done, is doing, and will do (tomorrow's devotion) in your life to draw others to Himself.

Lord, I thank You that You're not some far-off, unapproachable deity that someone has made up. You're real and alive! You're with me every moment! So, help me to hear Your voice, to really listen, and obey. In Your timing, allow me to share my life in You with another.

Other passages for your prayerful consideration:
Ps 23:1-6, 46:1; Prv 6:20-23; Mt 6:11, 33-34, 28:18-20; Jn 10:1-18; Acts 16:6-10; 2 Cor. 6:2; Heb 3:13, 4:6-11, 13:5b-6, 8

Journaling: What's the Lord doing in your life currently? What are you learning? What are you gleaning from the Word? How is He <u>speaking</u> to you? How are you sensing His leading? How is Jesus providing for you?

Day Eighteen:
What's in My Future with Jesus?

> *. . .In all (these) things we are more than conquerors through Him who loved (& loves) us. I am convinced that neither death nor life, neither angels nor demons, neither the present nor the future (& certainly not the past) nor any powers, neither height nor depth, nor anything else in all creation, will be able to separate us from the love of God that is in Christ Jesus our Lord.* (Rom 8:37-39)

I was in a conversation with a young Mormon elder one day discussing salvation and heaven. (More on sharing with Mormons on Day 36) "It's like being in a pit. You can't get out on your own, and the Lord saves you by throwing you a rope. You tie it around your waist and He pulls you up."

"Well, I think He'd throw down a ladder," was his response. He couldn't understand the concept of God imparting righteousness to us through faith in Jesus as the basis of His relationship with us. In the Mormon religion, you work your way to the highest level of heaven – godhood. I so wanted him to be free.

Pleadingly, I replied, "But, your legs are broken from the fall."

His look was blank. Then, his face got red, and he blurted out, "I feel sorry for you, because when you get to heaven all you'll have is Christ!" He did get it, and that was his response!

I was <u>almost</u> speechless: "And, that's a bad thing?"

We know that we will never really die. Death will simply be a door through which we walk from this temporal life into eternity. We actually know quite a bit about heaven thanks to the Bible. I'm sure looking forward to it! Sometimes I think today would be a great one for the Lord's return, but then I find myself asking for just one more disciple first. **We may have a lot of future with God before heaven! We may not, so there is an urgency** to get the message out, understood, received, and lived.

"Jesus does not want to be Number One in your life." You could feel the air being sucked out of the room as the audience for The Jeremiah People heard this seemingly blasphemous statement. This was a time when we were all making our lists: God first, then family, work, church. . . . They had our attention and after a pause said, **"Jesus wants to BE your life!"** For our good, He wants to be Number One in every relationship, in every priority, and in every activity. He is the Center, the Vine, the Source, the Way, Truth, and Life.

So where are you in life's journey? Are you a student? Do you already have a career? Are you married; single? Are you near retirement or retired? Your story is still unfolding. **The way that you're allowing God to direct your life as you look ahead is a very important part of your story. Your future is the faith part.** The past and the present fall into the realm of knowledge. Because you've experienced God's hand in your life, your faith has grown. So you're approaching the future with confidence, anticipation, and excitement. **This is also a very interesting part of your story – all the chapters yet to be completed.**

You have a circle of influence – eight to fifteen people – your *oikos*; Greek for "extended household." They are very interested in you; your past, present, and future. **Blending the story of Jesus with yours will be natural and therefore very effective when God gives you an opportunity to share the gospel, because Jesus IS your life.**

Lord, my life is in Your hands. I have willingly given it to You. You were working with me even before I knew it. I trust You with my future. I want to learn to share my story and blend it with Yours. May it bless those who hear. Thank You, Jesus.

Other passages for your prayerful consideration:
Ps 37:3:3-6; Prv 3:4-6, 16:3, 21:1; Jer 29:11-13

Journaling: In your journaling today, consider the future. Are you already on track to complete something you've started? Is there an unfulfilled "Jesus Dream" in your heart? Talk with God about it. Write it down.

Day Nineteen:
I Can Blend My Story with His.

You do not want to leave too, do you?" Jesus asked the twelve. Simon Peter answered Him, "Lord, to whom shall we go? You have the words of eternal life. We believe and know that You are the Holy One of God." (Jn 6:67-68)

T om drove a truck for a living. He loved his work for he was able to spend a lot of time talking with the Lord. Once, when he had a cold, he popped a cough drop in his mouth and offered the Lord one. Then, he caught himself and said aloud, "Oh, You don't need a cough drop!" He shook his head and caught himself again! "Whoa! What did I just do!?" My friend's relationship with the Lord was very close and comfortable. He laughed at himself when he told this story, but I've always remembered it. It calls me to ask myself how aware of God's presence am I as I go through my day? **Blending my story with that of Jesus should be the easiest thing in the world to do.** After all, He is my life! And yet, I can go on and on in a conversation without His name coming up. It could go something like this:

"Hey Dave, how's it goin'?"

"Good, with you?"

"Good. So, what's new?"

"Not much. Got a new grill for Father's Day."

"That's cool."

"Blah, blah, blah . . . ." God provided me with a new BBQ grill and I didn't even give Him the glory! Should every conversation include the Lord? The key to when and how to bring the Lord into a conversation is simple. We need to be mindful of His presence so that "God-talk" is not contrived; rather it's natural. **When the Holy Spirit gives the opportunity, rest assured it's with someone He's already been speaking to.** We simply blend His story with ours. The conversation above could have gone naturally like this:

"Hey Dave, how's it goin'?"

"God's been good to me. What's up with you?" Now, my friend is talking about himself (something most of us love to do), and I listen and respond appropriately.

"God gave me a new grill for Father's Day."

"God did, huh? Good thing it didn't hit ya on the head when He dropped it out of the sky!"

It's funny; I chuckle. "Almost did! Actually, the Lord put it on my wife's heart to get me a new one. I love it! I can cook for a crowd now! Hey, why don't you guys come over tomorrow night? I'll throw on some steaks."

Later, I bathe "tomorrow night" in prayer. "Lord, allow the conversation to flow naturally to You." The message that comes out is, "God loves me and cares about my life. He loves and is concerned about you too. . . ." **You don't have to push God on anyone.** You're growing in relationship and having a conversation with a friend you may have had for years, or with a new friend. **Trust God's timing. He'll pave the way.**

I've been privileged to blend my story with His with new and old friends, with family, and new acquaintances. I'm still learning to **wait and be ready for "let it happen" moments.** If I relax and think of my life as being inseparable from Jesus, He will come up naturally. Be aware of His presence and working in and through your life. Pray for opportunities to share His love and touch someone that perhaps no one else could reach.

Jesus, I want my life to flow from Yours naturally. Help me to live it in a way that includes You in my thoughts, actions, and words that others may come to know You as I do. Thank You, Lord.

God stories for your prayerful consideration:
Gn 47:7-10; Ru (All); 1 Sm 17:32-58; Est (all); Is. 6:1-8; Jer 1:4-9; Dn 3:13-30, 6:13-28; Mt 9:9-13; Mk 14:21-22; Lk 1:1-4; 1ˢᵗ Jn 1:1-5; Acts 11:1-18, 26:1-32

Journaling: Describe your relationship with Jesus in terms of closeness. Ask God for wisdom and guidance to be even more aware of His 24/7 presence.

Day Twenty:
I Will Walk in the Spirit.

. . .in this world we are like Him. . . (1 Jn 4:17)

"Hey Sam!" From across the street, Sam the Recycle Man looked up. I waved and he came over.

"The president says, 'Recycle,' and that's what I do," he had told me the first time we met while on one of my walks.

"Hey, we're serving a meal here today. Have you eaten yet?" Sam was our first guest at the Community Meal served every Saturday from our church's Fellowship Hall. He was our only guest that day. But now, on Thanksgiving, over 100 people are served! Every Saturday, some 40, 50, 60, or more people have a place to relax, fellowship, and enjoy a meal. This is because one precious lady, Jovi Benavides, decided to be "Jesus-with-skin-on." Jovi had a dream and it has grown to be a reflection of the love of Jesus in our community. They come, eat, and get clothes from a "closet" on the campus. They hear God's Word (on a voluntary, not mandatory basis). Some come to know the Lord. They are all encouraged in their faith. The ministry is still growing. Now we're looking at having showers available on site. Most don't come to the church on Sunday. Church for our Community Meal guests falls on Saturday as we attempt to, **in this world, be like Him**. (1 Jn 4:17)

I spoke with Sam again a little while back. "The Lord is MY Shepherd!" he said, pointing to the sky.

You've been focusing this week on your spiritual journey. It is your story blended with the Jesus story. We need to also learn others' stories, like Jovi's and Sam's, because we don't know until the Spirit reveals it to us just whose story needs to be told and heard in order for the listener to be drawn to Christ. **Spiritual journeys begin with the Spirit's wooing.** *No one can come to Me unless the Father draws him, and I will raise him up at the last day.* (Jn 6:44) Once we've submitted to the love and lordship of Jesus, it is the Spirit Who teaches and guides us. . . .*The Counselor, the Holy Spirit, Whom the Father will send in My Name, will teach you all things; . . . when He, the Spirit of Truth, comes, He will guide you into all truth.* (Jn 14:26 and 16:13) . . .*Those who are led by the Spirit of God are sons* (and daughters) *of God.* (Rom 8:14) **We need big spiritual ears, and He will teach us what our hands are to do, where our feet are to go, and what our mouths are to speak.** The secret of being comfortable in our going, doing, and speaking is the listening.

Let's revisit the call of Jesus, which as His fully devoted followers (disciples), has become our call. *The Spirit of the Lord is on Me, because He has anointed Me to preach good news to the poor. He has sent Me to proclaim freedom for the prisoners and recovery of sight for the blind, to release the oppressed, and proclaim the year of the Lord's favor.* (Lk 4:18-19) **This is not a call to action OR proclamation; it is a call to action <u>AND</u> proclamation!** It is not a call for 95% to demonstrate the gospel and 5% to proclaim the gospel. It is a call for **ALL** of us to do both **as led by the Holy Spirit with our own gifts, personality and passion.**

"I'm no good at showing mercy!"

"I'm not good at talking!"

Which of the above declarations fits you the best? You may be really good at declaring the Good News and not so good at showing the love of Jesus, or vice versa. That is why we must allow ourselves to be led by the Spirit. **God is calling us to do what we're good at <u>and</u> what we're not so good at, by His Spirit, with His leading, wisdom, and strength.** So, yes, we will step out of our comfort zones but not so far that we'll have to make ourselves into something we're not. **God's strength is made perfect in our weakness.** (1 Cor 1:18-31)

Moses didn't feel equipped to guide the Israelites out of Egypt; he needed the assurance of God's leading. *If Your Presence does not go with us, do not send us up from here.* But **God had promised, *"My Presence will go with you, and I will give you rest."*** (Ex 33:14-15) Remember, Jesus has promised to be with us always! (Mt 28:18-20)

Lord, teach me to act and to speak by Your Spirit's leading. Be glorified my life. Thank You.

Other passages for your prayerful consideration:
Mt 3:11; Jn 20:19-23; Acts 1:4-8, 2:1-4

Journaling: Review your story. Whittle down each part. You'll want to be able to share it in just 2-3 minutes.

Day Twenty-One:
Spiritual Disciplines: It's about "Want To" not "Have To."

> *. . .Live by the Spirit, and you will not gratify the desires of the flesh.*
> (Gal 5:16)

The room was filled with tension. Men were yelling at the tops of their voices. "To be saved, these Gentile followers of Jesus must be circumcised and obey the Law of Moses!"

"No! God has purified their hearts and saved them by grace through faith!"

"They must demonstrate their faith by obeying the Law!"

"No man can be justified by obeying the law! By trying to do so, they cannot be saved!"

And so the heated discussion went in the early days of the ministries of Paul and the other apostles. Finally, it was James, the brother of Jesus and the author of the New Testament letter that bears his name, who brought the resolution to the floor. *It is my judgment that we should not make it difficult for Gentiles who are turning to God. Instead, we should write to them, telling them to abstain from food polluted by idols, from sexual immorality, from the meat of strangled animals and from blood.* (Acts 15:19-20)

Paul delivered this letter, no doubt, with much joy! Still today, we find ourselves setting up rules of conduct for ourselves and others. Friends, there is only one rule for a disciple of Jesus Christ: **Listen to the Voice of the Holy Spirit and oBEy.** Remember, the word "BE" is the center of the word "oBEy." This week, plus weeks one and two, focuses on who we are in Christ, because we must "BE" before we can oBEy with a right heart, so our stories will have an impact. "Dad, just BE the branch." (Jn 15:1-8 – See Day Two.)

Christianity is not a "have to" religion; it is a "want to" relationship. We do not do good works to get to God; we demonstrate the love of God as a response to His love for us. We don't share our stories and the love of God with people because we have to; rather, we do so because we can't help ourselves. We're acting and speaking, and even thinking, from the position of our preciousness to God as shown through Jesus. We're partaking of His nature. We have His passion for people. His purposes have become our perspective. We want to and do allow God to use our gifts, personalities, and passion to accomplish His will in helping people who are lost and need to be reconciled. This is who we are!

The Fruit of the Spirit has nine facets to it: love, joy, peace, patience, kindness, goodness, faithfulness, gentleness, and self control. **Can gardeners *make* fruit grow?** No, what do they do? They turn the soil, enrich it, plant seeds, water, and tend the weeds, and the **fruit just grows naturally.** That's how we are. **We are God's orchard!** We're enriched by reading, studying, and meditating on the Word of God; we pray through the Spirit of God. In other words, **we eat the Living Bread, drink the Living Water, grow, and bear fruit. There's no "have to" here; it's natural.** The goal of the Christian life is for the spiritual to become natural as the old nature with its fears and lusts dies. Friends, this is what makes your faith in Jesus contagious! This is the abundant life! We must BE in order to DO! "That's why we're called human BEings, not human DOings." (Tony, a Community Meal guest) "To live is to choose, but to choose well, you must know who you are and what you stand for, where you want to go and why you want to get there." (Former student, Melissa)

The rest of this devotional is about tools for you to use, but they would be useless without the living principles of these first three weeks. Weeks One-Three are the foundation. Now let's build on it.

Lord, You know me; You made me. Help me to live a life that honors You with the awareness of Your presence and anointing. Work in and through me for Your glory. Thank You, Jesus.

Other passages for your prayerful consideration:
Jn 10:1-18; Rom 3:10-8:39; 1 Cor 2:9-16; Gal 5:1-26; Eph 1:13-2:10, 5:1-20; Phil 2:5-11; Col 3:1-17; 2 Pt 1:3-11; 1 Jn 1:5-2:2

Journaling: Make a continuum. At one end of the line write "WANT TO"; at the other end write "HAVE TO". Think about your Christian life. Place an "X" on the line that shows where you are. Ask the Lord to show you how to live more out of "WANT TO" and less out of "HAVE TO".

Section II
Letting the Living Water Flow

Week 4

The Gospel Message

Day Twenty-Two:
What Are the Four Spiritual Laws?

 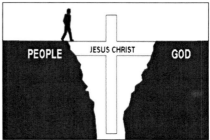

. . .The one who looks intently into the perfect law that gives freedom, and continues to do this, not forgetting what he's heard, but doing it—he will be blessed in what he does. (Jas 1:25)

Hakim closed his eyes and waited for the crack of the gun. He was crouched, feet in the starting blocks, muscles twitching, ready for the race of his life. Bang! He had a great jump. A glance to his left, then the right told Hakim he was out in front. He listened for the sounds of the runners behind him. Strangely, he heard nothing. Something didn't feel right. Hakim looked back and slowed. Where were the other runners? He looked up at the huge clock on the stadium marquee. Ten o'clock. Ten o'clock? Hakim had slowed to a trot. He looked around. Had he imagined the sound of the start gun? Had he been so focused that he didn't notice that he was the only runner lined up? This wasn't the right track. His race was at eleven o'clock. Hakim shook himself and sat up in bed. He laughed out loud! He had dreamed that he was in the wrong race, on the wrong track!

When it comes to God and religion in general, there are almost as many ideas as there are people. Many are on the wrong track and in the wrong race. "Is there a God? If so, does He expect anything of me?" "If there is a God, why doesn't He do something about the mess the world is in?" "If I wanted to talk to God, how would I do it?" "Which religion is right?" **The Four Spiritual Laws simply help you to explain how to get into the right race on the right track.** In the mid-1960's, Bill Bright identified these principles to help the believer understand salvation and answer questions people may have from a scriptural perspective. I encourage you to meditate on these "laws" until you know them well. (Verses for each below)

1. **God is love.** He loves you and others. He wants a love relationship with each of us. That's why the Great Commandments teach us to love God and our "neighbor" as ourselves.
2. **There is a problem: sin separates people from God.** Sin is simply breaking God's moral laws summed up in the Ten Commandments. God is perfectly holy, but of all the people who have ever lived, only Jesus Christ was perfect.

God requires that we turn away from sin (repent), but even though we try, we can never be perfectly righteous.

3. **God provided a solution through Jesus Christ.** He alone is the bridge between sinful man and a holy God. We cannot earn God's favor or become right with the Lord on our own. Through Jesus, we can receive righteousness as God's gift. When He died on the cross, Jesus took the penalty for our sin and God's justice was satisfied. At the same time His love for us was demonstrated. God will forgive our sin when we ask Him in prayer (just talking with God) and, by faith accept Jesus as our personal Savior and Lord.

4. **Receive salvation as a gift and begin to walk by faith.** God doesn't promise a life free of problems, but when we tell Him that we want to accept Jesus personally, turn from sin, and live for His glory, He hears us. By grace, He makes us His own. Through the Holy Spirit, He comes into our heart and makes it His home. He gives us faith as a gift, and we can know that our sins are forgiven. We are "born again" into His family. He begins cleansing our hearts. His promises are sure. We know God accepts us, and that we will spend eternity in heaven.

Lord, Your gospel is simple. Help me to know it so well that it becomes a part of me, so that I can naturally share it with someone in a way that they too can know You. Thank You, Lord.

Other passages for your prayerful consideration:
Law 1: Mt 22:36-40; Jn 3:16-17; Rom 5:8
Law 2: Ex 20:1-17; Rom 3:10, 19-25, 6:23
Law 3: Jn 14:1-6; 1 Cor 15:1-6; 2 Cor 5:17, 21; Eph 2:8-10
Law 4: Jn 1:12 & 13, 3:3-8, 14:23; Rom 8:14-16, 10:9-13; Rv 3:20
Assurance: 1 Jn 1:5-2:2, 3:1-3, 4:13-18, 5:9-15

Journaling: Carry these verses with you: highlighted in your pocket New Testament, your phone, or on note cards; review them often. All conversations about spiritual things will flow into one or more of the "laws".

Day Twenty-Three:
How Can I Apply this Basis for Salvation Personally?

. . .I am not ashamed because I know Whom I have believed, and am convinced that He is able to guard what I have entrusted to Him for that day. (2 Tm 1:12)

The voice was a soft, sweet whisper, like a cool evening breeze at the close of a sizzling day. With a hint of something better to offer, it asked, "How do you know you're 'saved'? How do you know the Bible is true? If there is a God, why would He bother with you?" Suddenly, a rush of pleasurable thoughts entered my mind: images of popularity, wealth, and all that would come with it. I asked myself, "Am I serving God for nothing?" Heaven seemed to be silent. I bowed my head and waited. The first voice persisted. "You're a good person. Do you really want to be just another religious hypocrite? You don't need it. Take life by the tail!" I breathed deeply, head still bowed, and waited for something deeper in my spirit to arise.

Have you been there? My first mentor, Mel Brewer, at 65 with years of serving the Lord, once testified that he'd heard that "voice." "How do you know you're saved?" With a very serious expression, he shared his response. "Well, let's see. . . ." He said **he reviewed in his mind the facts of biblical salvation.** He didn't turn to warm, fuzzy feelings; he turned to the Word. He believed that there was a God who loved him, Who had proven it by sending His own Son to live, die for our sins, and rise in victory on the third day. He recognized that he was a sinner in need of God's mercy and grace. He believed that Jesus had taken his punishment on the cross and that God accepted this as the penalty for his sins and those of the whole world. He had not rejected the gift of God but had repented of sin and committed his life to serving the Lord. "Yes! Yes, I do know I'm saved! Get behind me Satan!" The color in Mel's cheeks returned. I'd seen it scores of times as the anointing came over him to teach. He began to worship right there on the spot. We, his students, just joined in, praising our God and Savior! I thought later, "If that temptation can come to Brother Brewer, it can come to anyone. If it hits me, I'll handle it like he did."

❑ I stand alone on the Word of God, the B-I-B-L-E—BIBLE! ❑ (unknown)

Have you heard the **train illustration**? In it, the engine is the Word of God. The next connecting car is Faith. The caboose is Feelings. I love it when I'm feeling great, but that train will run without the last car! **The Bible is the most scrutinized book in the world. It has been proven to be reliable and true.** I have the witness of its truth in my own heart. Why do you think Satan worked so hard to keep it from us? Just a few hundred years ago, people were being burned at the stake just because they wanted everyone to have opportunity to read it for themselves. It's still banned in some countries. In free countries, the Bible sits on the shelf, in many homes, collecting dust. It can only be taught as literature in U. S. public schools. **Your enemy doesn't want you to know the Bible and come to rely upon its truth.** I could go on and on about cultic "translations," misinterpretations, adaptations, outright lies. . .but friends, my old mentor Mel Brewer said it right. He taught us, **"The Bible is the handle by which we get hold of God."**

    You must be sure of your own salvation before you can share your faith confidently with others. When the enemy comes at you with his lies, say what Jesus did. *"Be gone Satan!"* (Mt 4:10) *Submit yourselves to God. Resist the devil, and he will flee from you. Come near to God and He will come near to you.* (Jas 4:7-8)

Lord, praise You for revealing Yourself and the truth of salvation to me through Your Son, Jesus Christ. Help me to share my faith with confidence. Thank You, Lord.

Other passages for your prayerful consideration:
Assurance verses - Day 22; Rom 8:1-4, 28-39

Journaling: Review the Four Spiritual Laws from a personal standpoint. Write about how each one was/is applicable in your own life.

Day Twenty-Four:
Outreach through Service and the Word Need a Marriage.

*And whatever you do, whether **in word or in deed**, do it all in the Name of the Lord Jesus, giving thanks to God the Father through Him.* (Col 3:17)

"This week we had very low temperatures for South Florida (35 degrees). We are not used to cold and the homeless find open areas to bed down, mostly without any shielding from the elements. The shelters fill up fast here in cool weather and with a cold front bearing down on us, we made a plea on Facebook for donations to buy blankets, sleeping bags, socks and food. In less than 24 hours we had $340. Sports Authority made us a great deal and I bought all the polar fleece blankets they had (30) and from thrift stores we found sleeping bags, blankets and coats. We also bought packages of socks and gloves. We got some food to hand out a meal with each set-up. We were able to help 45 people!"

Wow, what a demonstration of God's love! . . . What if I told you this was not done for the sake of the gospel? It's true. I took this testimony, verbatim, from an atheist website by Ken Loukinen, President, Florida Atheists and Secular Humanists and South Florida Regional Director, American Atheists. **There are lots of individuals and groups who do good works.** I'm thankful for them, but when the Church shows God's love without telling people about His salvation it's like telling a story and skipping the end.

Let me offer another scenario: A young woman reads in Luke 4 where it says that the mission of Jesus was to proclaim good news to the poor. So she travels to an area in Africa where a famine has left thousands dying of thirst, hunger, and exposure. A pulpit is found. This saint opens the Bible and preaches with all her might! The message of the love of God and His salvation through Jesus is passionately proclaimed. People respond to her altar call but many die before making it all the way forward. Some die while they're praying to receive Jesus. Others live, barely, but they are holding dying and dead children. No physical needs are met. . . . Ridiculous? Yes! I know this is an exaggeration, but I'm sure you get the point! **Proclamation without demonstration is like a sandwich with only bread!** Where are the mayo, mustard, lettuce, tomato, avocado, meat, and cheese?

The goal is not to just do good deeds.
Nor is it to just proclaim the Gospel with words.
The goal is "faith expressing itself through love." (Gal 5:6b)

Let me address gifting. Evangelists <u>tell</u> about Jesus, and those with the gift of mercy <u>show</u> His love, right? Yes, but **the evangelist can learn to show love, which will pave the way for his words. The merciful can learn to be ready to share words when their acts of kindness open ears. Must there be an either/or scenario with all the proclaimers on one side and all the demonstrators on the other?** The natural evangelist can learn from the one with the gift of mercy: Your message will be more effective when people's needs are met. Those who are good at demonstrating God's love can learn to share their own personal Jesus stories with people when **God opens the doors of opportunity.** To see the Great Commission fulfilled, there must be a unified effort by a unified community full of love for one another and for those outside the fold. (Jn 13:34-35, 17:20-21) We **_all_** need to be . . . *ready to give an answer, gently and respectfully, to anyone. . .* (1 Pt 3:15). We can **_all_** be planting seeds, watering, and enjoying the harvest as we **show and proclaim** the Gospel of Jesus Christ!

Lord, show me if I am on one side of the pendulum's swing or the other, and help me to be balanced. Show me how to demonstrate and proclaim Your Gospel as You give opportunity. Thank You, Lord.

Other passages for your prayerful consideration:
Mt 4:23-25, 9:35-38, 10:5-8, 11:1-6; Mk 1:21-28, 2:1-12; Lk 4:18-19, 7:1-17; Jn 4:1-42, 9:1-41, 11:1-44; Acts 2:42-47, 3:1-26, 16:25-34, 19:8-12; Gal 5:6b

Journaling: A quote attributed to St. Francis is often stated: "Preach the Gospel at all times and **IF** necessary, use words." In keeping with his teachings, **WHEN** would be more appropriate. Where would you place yourself on a continuum with WORD at one end and SERVICE at the other? The Lord will help you to find a balance.

Day Twenty-Five:
What's Love Got to Do with It? – EVERYTHING!

The only thing that counts is faith expressing itself through love.
(Gal 5:6b)

S lam! The whole house rattled, but not as much as my nerves, when my stepdad stormed out. My heart was full of fear and anger all the time toward him. There was a constant yelling, demanding, coming home drunk, and complaining to Mom about the normal bills while it was okay for him to stay out all hours drinking, fighting, and gambling. We never knew when he would explode. It was like a sword waiting to fall. I was glad when he left, but this night was different, though not better. Bam, bam, bam! "Let me in!" he hollered, having forgotten something. Mom went to unlock the door and just as she did, he hit it and it flew open cracking her hard above the eye. There was blood everywhere. I literally wanted to kill him! Would this go on forever? How could she stand him? For thirty years, Mom demonstrated the love of God to my stepdad. Finally, after the children were all gone, he "graduated" from alcohol to cocaine. When he began cutting it at home and going through money like crazy to pay for his habit, she got scared enough to say, "Enough."

After the divorce, my dad (he was the only one I knew growing up, but that's another story) moved in with a cousin who knew the Lord. He was humbled enough to listen to her and eventually went to her church. **One night, he felt the Spirit of Christ drawing him, and as he walked forward down the aisle, Dad felt that Spirit enter his heart.** When I heard, I could hardly believe it! You may recall how the disciples felt about Saul/Paul at first? (Acts 9:13, 26) I had tried to share Christ with him; even bought him a nice leather-bound Bible three years earlier. With Dad's salvation, a real relationship began between us. I got hugs and kisses on the cheek that I never got as a boy. Dad became gentle and humble. He asked me to baptize him, and after he passed on, I got his Bible. In the back of the book of Acts, he had briefly written in his own handwriting the four spiritual laws. My dad, the hardest man I've ever known, is in heaven! How could he not have come to know Jesus? My believing **Mom had shown and told him of God's love** for all those years, and even after the split. They couldn't reunite – Dad was afraid of hurting her again; Mom was afraid too. But **she had enough faith to love him to the Lord.** My mom was not a Bible scholar. She didn't talk about Jesus with everyone she met. She just faithfully stuck with the tough assignment that God gave her. We mentioned the sandwich of 1 Cor 12, 13, and 14 before. Bottom line: **Love must be the motivation for all of our actions and words, and it is supernaturally available to us. God's love in and through us is what the Holy Spirit will use to draw our dear ones to Jesus.** Please read 1 Cor 13 again. Meditate especially on the description of love in verses 4-8a. Think and pray through all your relationships and line your heart up with God's Word. **Tap into the Source of love that will express itself through your faith in Jesus Christ.**

One last word of caution: my dad was very scary but was not physically abusive to my mom or us kids. Love and forgiveness do not require staying in an abusive situation. Love is not the same thing as trust. Love is free; trust is earned. Love can allow trust to be earned again. God can heal anything. The important thing is to be in His will and grace. No two situations are the same. **God's leading will always include love.** It is the key for any witness; for life itself. *God is love.* (1 Jn 4:7)

*Lord, You loved me so much that you sent Jesus to live, die for my sins, and rise in victory. **I must have Your love working in and through me if I am to be Your disciple.** Please baptize me in Your love and help me to express it in my circles of influence. Thank You, Lord.*

Other passages for your prayerful consideration:
Gn 45:1-15; Prv 3:3-6; Mt 5:43-48; 1 Cor. 13; Eph 5:1-2; 1 Thes 1:3; 1 Tm 4:12; Heb 10:19-25; Jas 2:8-13; 1 Jn 4:7-21

Journaling: Write a love letter from God to you and a reply from you back to Him.

Day Twenty-Six:
"Make It Happen" . . . "Let It Happen"

The wind blows wherever it pleases. You hear its sound, but you cannot tell where it comes from or where it is going. So it is with everyone born of the Spirit. (Jn 3:8)

Make It Happen – A nice young couple lived around the corner from us. I just knew they needed to know Jesus so we invited them over for dinner with the purpose in mind of leading them to Christ. It was a long time ago, but I'm pretty sure they did pray the "sinner's prayer" before they escaped. Afterward however, we were never able to make contact again; a relationship never developed. If discipleship occurred, it was without our influence. **Spiritual mugging isn't effective.**

Let It Happen – Our son, Jeff, was about seven and played with little Porfi across the street. He invited him to Sunday School. One day, not long afterwards, his sister, Novelta, came over to visit. "How do you get Jesus into your heart, Dona?" My wife shared the simple four spiritual laws and led her in a prayer of repentance and commitment to Jesus. She and her mom began attending church with Porfi, and all of them accepted Christ as Savior and Lord. **Nurturing relationships and naturally sharing faith is something that any of us can do with more effectiveness than "make it happen" activity.**

There are times when Make It Happen may be appropriate. I've experienced a sense of urgency that was "prompted by the Holy Spirit." The key is "prompted by the Holy Spirit." Here's a good rule:

Before saying or doing anything that is done
in an effort to win the lost and make disciples, PRAY.

Most of us, if not all, are more comfortable with Let It Happen. Our theme verse, 1 Pt 3:15, tells us to share our faith *with gentleness and respect.* That's hard to do if you're trying to force things.

Let It Happen living is good for application in all of our lives, yet 1 Pt 3:15 says, *"be ready?"* "B*e ready"* is a Make it Happen exhortation. Why? Because Make It Happen prepares us so we are equipped to live our lives in Let It Happen mode. The athlete trains and practices; then he or she is ready for the race or the game. The student studies hard preparing him or herself for a future career. A pastor prepares his sermon. A teacher prepares lesson plans. **Preparation sets us free when the unexpected comes.** Here's an example: The teacher is in the middle of a math lesson. A butterfly comes into the classroom through a window. It's time for science! Her lesson plans have set her free to take advantage of a teachable moment. **Our preparation readies us when God opens doors to share His love in word and in deed.**

So, Make it Happen is fine for learning to tell your Jesus story, memorizing some gospel verses from the Bible, and being so familiar with the four spiritual laws that you can naturally navigate any spiritual discussion. Pray for your loved ones. Be sensitive to the Holy Spirit's nudge, so that when He gives opportunity you'll **recognize the Let it Happen moment**, and be ready to share the gospel.

Lord, please help me to follow Your leading and not jump out ahead of You. Nor do I want to be so laid back that I miss opportunities that You provide. Help me to be ready to share Your message with actions and words in a timely and effective way. Thank You, Lord.

Other passages for your prayerful consideration:
Prv 19:21; Mt 4:18-20, 6:33-34; Jn 6:44-48; Rom 1:17, 8:14-15, 10:9-15; 1 Thes 5:16-19; 2 Tm 2:15, 3:14-17; Jude 1:17-25

Journaling: Think about times when you have been in Make It Happen mode and other times when you've been in Let It Happen mode. Ask the Lord to help you apply both appropriately in the future.

Day Twenty-Seven:
I Have Circles of Influence.

. . . Even His Own brothers did not believe in Him. (Jn 7:5)

Jesus said to them, "Only in his hometown, among his relatives and in his own house a prophet is without honor." (Mk 6:4)

"I told ya, stop hasslin' me with that Jesus stuff!" Andy went to a Christian school where he had accepted Christ as his Savior. Now, he wanted everyone to know, especially his family. But whenever he tried to talk with his dad, he just got into trouble. Andy had been adopted. He was very grateful, and his parents had given him a life any boy would envy. He lived in a large house and had his own room. The house was on a lot of property where they could ride dirt bikes and go-carts. They had a big swimming pool, and when Andy wasn't tearing over hills on his bike, he was in the water. Yet, as nice as his life was, he couldn't be happy unless his parents came to know the Lord. He kept trying to share his faith, as gently as possible.

One night, he overheard his dad and mom talking. "Get rid of that kid!"

"We can't do that! What would people say?" the wife argued.

"I don't care! He's drivin' me nuts with that Jesus stuff! Wouldn't his friend's parents take 'im?" The next thing Andy knew, he was packing his clothes. He was happy in his new home because they all shared his faith. He missed his life of privilege as his new family could not afford all the nice things he had before, but even more, he regretted that his first adoptive parents did not put their faith in Christ. Andy continued to have hope and kept praying.

This may shock you, but the above story is true. Only the name "Andy" is made up. I will not try to deceive you. **Those closest to you may be the hardest to reach.** However, please recall the story of my stepdad. (Day 25) *With God, all things are possible.* (Lu. 1:37) **Our job is to be faithful, and leave the rest to God.** Some who are close to you may be very open. Others will need to observe your behavior, and you may need to pray for a long time before they are won. You're making yourself ready if the Lord opens a door, but perhaps the message will have to come through someone else. Until then, demonstrate the love of God; be faithful to Him, and pray. You may have heard people say, "Well, at least I can pray." Brother Brewer taught us that "prayer is the MOST you can do, not the least." Remember, no one comes to the Lord unless he or she is drawn by the Spirit. (Jn 6:44)

You know the old cliché: "If you aim at nothing, you'll be sure to hit it." So, I encourage you to **make a list of those in your circles of influence.** There will probably be 8-15 people with whom you have the most contact. You will also have a wider circle of other friends, work associates, service people like the checker at your store (although, she could easily make the inner circle), etc. And, you have even a wider circle of acquaintances and those whom you seldom see. These circles are fluid; people move from one to another. (Jesus had an inner circle of Peter, James, and John.

The next circle was the rest of the twelve. Then, there were seventy that He sent out, and finally there were the crowds.)

Make a list of those closest to you. **Love and pray for each person on it!** Loving will not always be easy; let God love through you. Pray with faith! They may push you away, but they can't escape your prayers. Stay as prepared as you can be. Journal progress and setbacks, and keep your list updated. You will see God working with, in and through you!

Father, You are the One Who draws people to Yourself, and I know You are faithful. Help me to be faithful too. Use me with the people in my circles of influence, indirectly and directly. I know You love them as much as You do me. Thank You, Lord.

Other passages for your prayerful consideration:
Hos 2:19-20; Jn 4:34-38; 1 Thes 5:23-24

Journaling: "Oikos" is the Greek word for "extended household" (Day 18). Make your list of 8 – 15 people. Pray for them. Ask God to show you how to love each one in a new way and put it into practice.

Day Twenty-Eight:
Love. . .Pray. . .Love. . .Pray. . .Love. . .Pray. . .Love. . .

. . .If. . .I have not love . . .I have nothing . . .I am nothing . . .I gain nothing . . ." (1 Cor 1:1-3 paraphrase) *"Do not be anxious about anything, but in everything, by prayer and petition, with thanksgiving, present your requests* (loved ones) *to God."* (Phil 4:6)

I was sitting with friends in the University of Nevada, Las Vegas (UNLV) Commons and out of the blue came the inner voice. "Go and share with Dr. Pasturk."

I was gripped by fear! "What? He'll make mincemeat out of me! Lord, this sounds like "make it happen." Couldn't You have him come over to me?" But God's call was persistent. Dr. Pasturk had been a philosophy professor of mine about seven years earlier. He was brilliant and had a Russian accent that was intimidating. Reluctantly, I obeyed. I reintroduced myself. Like a computer, he had me – total recall. I thought, "I'm dead!"

"Ahh, Mr. Kachele, what to you is the meaning of life?"

Fear left room for only one thought: "Well, Jesus said, 'I am the way and the truth and the life. No one comes to the Father except through me.'" (Jn 14:6)

"Ah-ha, then to you. . . ("Oh boy, here it comes - the hamburger grinder!") Jesus is the way, or the paathh."

"Yeah," was my intelligent reply.

"And to you, Jesus encompasses allll truuthh."

"Yeah," I said again, sharp as a whip!

"And to you, allll of liiffe consists in Jesus."

"Yeah." I was on a roll! "Here it comes," I thought, cringing. Suddenly, the doctor's expression changed. It was no longer confident, but questioning. He began to stumble over his words and talk about his Catholic upbringing. The next thing I knew, he was making excuses and had to go. I sat there dumbfounded, having contributed only one Bible verse and three "Yeahs" to the conversation. Another passage came to mind. *But God chose the foolish things of the world* (me) *to shame the wise. . .the strong* . . . (1 Cor 1:20-31). I never saw my former professor again after that encounter, but I loved him and he remained in my prayers for years. God's faithful; I hope Dr. Pasturk is with Him.

I could have told you many stories about times when I totally blew it. **I've missed opportunities and said the wrong thing at the wrong time.** But the "Dr. Pasturks" and the failures have taught me something very important. I can still love and pray. God doesn't want *"anyone to perish."* (2 Pt 3:9)

Our enemy has many tools. His very often used and most worn is discouragement. It can render you ineffective, and depending on your personality, he may try to use it a lot or a little, but we've all experienced it. Even the Psalmist had to command his soul, over and over, not to be downhearted, and to bless the Lord. Psalm 103 is my favorite. It starts and ends, *Bless the Lord, O my soul.* (NASB)

None of us is perfect in hearing and obeying God's voice. We're growing. Two Peter 1:3-11 is a passage you will see more than once in this devotional/study guide. (See Day 2.) I don't have space to quote it all here. Read and meditate on it. In it you will find reassurance that if you *possess* godly qualities *in increasing measure, they will keep you from being ineffective and unproductive.* (vs. 8) *Let us not become weary in doing good, for at the proper time we will reap a harvest if we do not give up. Therefore, as we have opportunity, let us do good to all people. . . .* (Gal 6:9-10) **God uses ordinary people like you and me and He receives the glory only He deserves.**

Lord, show and speak love into my heart and then through me. When I miss opportunities or otherwise 'blow it,' use even my blunders for Your glory. Thank You for Your faithfulness.

Other passages for your prayerful consideration:
Lu. 18:1-8; Rom 8:26-28; 1 Cor 1:18-31, 13:1-8a

Journaling: Write about a time when you should have shared the Lord, but didn't. Give that person to the Lord. He is faithful. Was there ever a time when you were right on the money? If not, there will be.

Week 5

In Community: Fishing the Ponds

Day Twenty-Nine:
Visitors

. . .I was a stranger and you invited me in. . . (Mt 25:35)

The church was packed! Every seat was taken. The auditorium was so large that from the back you could hardly see the minister. You could only make out his multicolored stole, and his head and shoulders just above the pulpit. There was a festive air in the sanctuary. The service had already begun when the entrance at the back of the sanctuary slowly opened. In walked a bedraggled young man who fell to his knees behind the last pew. As I looked at him, wondering what to do, a figure of Christ appeared, very faint, but clear. Jesus gently put his hand on the man's head. The Savior remained standing with his head slightly bowed and His lips moving. The disheveled man didn't raise his face, but I could see tears running down his thin cheeks. The Bible says the Lord dwells in the praises of His people, but this Sunday He was behind the last row of worshipers. A whisper came to my heart. "This man needs Me with skin on." I quietly knelt beside him. As I did, the figure of Christ faded away. We stayed there with silent heads bowed until the end of the service.

The story above was inspired by a painting I saw once in a very nice church in an upper middle class neighborhood. Here are three possible endings:

1. "I gave him some money and wished him well."
2. "I took him to lunch where I told him about Christ's love for him, and he accepted Jesus as his Savior. Afterwards, I gave him a New Testament and we went our separate ways."
3. "I asked him how long it had been since he'd eaten. He told me 'a couple of days.' He allowed me to take him to lunch. Over our food, I got to know him a little. I learned his name and answered his questions about God as best I could. When we finished, I asked where he was staying and he nodded towards an alley. I took him home with me and he stayed with us for a little while. During that time, I was able to lead him to Christ. Today, the man is on his feet and serving the Lord."

Am I suggesting that we should take those living in the street into our homes? Conventional wisdom would say "no," but the Spirit may prompt us to do so. I will say that **"Visitor Follow-up" is not just a program; it's about people.** Many times, our visitors are Christians who are looking for a new church home. They could be believers who have just moved into the area and are seeking a place to worship and serve. Other times, however, they could be people with serious needs that we could help meet. No matter what, there are a few things to remember:

1. **God brings visitor(s) to us, and He loves them.** You don't need special training to love people; you're a partaker of God's nature. He will love through you. (Jn 6:44)
2. **God does not play favorites**, and neither should we. (Jas 2:2-13)
3. Our focus is to love God and people by winning the lost and growing disciples. Perhaps that starts with a nice Visitor's Packet, but our involvement should go further. **We need to have and show genuine interest.** This is not just the job of the greeter. It's why God put us in worshiping communities. We **all** need to be connected. Visitor Follow-up should not just be done by a committee. Not everyone can take a homeless person home, but some can. We can't all afford to take visitors out to lunch. Not everyone can spend a lot of time discipling new believers, but each of us could disciple one or perhaps a family. **God desires to and can accomplish His purposes** *through us.* (Eph 3:10-11)

Father, help us to be faithful with what and who You give to us. Thank You, Lord.

Other passages for your prayerful consideration:
Ps 146:7-9; Is 58:6-12; Mt 25:31-46; Lk 4:18-19; Jn 4:34-38; 1 Jn 4:16-211; Jude 1:22-23

Journaling: Think about your level of awareness of new people who come into your community of worship and service. Could you be more active in reaching out to new people? How?

Day Thirty:
Sunday School

Let the children come to Me, and do not hinder them, for the kingdom of heaven belongs to such as these. . . . anyone who will not receive the kingdom of God like a little child will never enter it. (Mk 10:14-15)

"Hey, throw it to me." She was a short, chubby, gray-haired lady, and when the boys playing ball in the street tossed one right to her, she didn't even come close to catching it. They laughed, and so did she. They laughed even harder as she went chasing after the ball. Her hair had been pulled up on top of her head but was partly falling down. She had on nylon socks that should have gone up to her knees under her dress, but one was rolled down to her ankle. What a sight. She came over to them with a broad smile on her face. "It's Sunday; what're you boys doin' here? Shouldn't you be in church?"

One of them replied, "Well, what about you, Lady? Shouldn't *you* be in church?"

Her grin never lessened as she said, "Well, I came lookin' for you. How about comin' to church with me? I've got milk and chocolate chip cookies."

They looked at one another. The oldest and obvious leader shrugged. "Ah, come on, what could it hurt? Chocolate Chips!" So off they trotted after the Sunday School Teacher.

Let's follow the "ideal" story a little further. The next week, the SS teacher pays a visit to each boy's home and introduces herself to their parents. Each home is happy to receive her when, later, she makes a call. She gets to know the families, and soon the parents and other children are attending church. Eventually, they all accept Christ, and their homes become havens of peace in the neighborhoods where they live. One boy grows up and becomes a successful business man who loves financing God's work, including his own personal involvement in it. Another becomes a pastor, another, a missionary, and another, an evangelist. Thousands of lives are touched through these men who in turn touch thousands of others with the power of the gospel, and it all started with a dedicated, discipling disciple – the Sunday School Teacher.

Yes, the story above is the ideal, but **there are many real life Sunday School testimonies.** Perhaps yours is one of them. If the Lord allows you to enter this area of ministry you will be among His choicest servants. A child's heart is soft and tender toward the Lord, and we have the promise in Prv 22:6 that if a child is trained up in the way he/she should go, he/she will not depart from it. **Current statistics reveal that 77% of all people who call themselves "born-again" Christians were saved by age 21(www.Barna.org 2004).** Stats go down from there. Here are a few other things to keep in mind as you consider being involved in this area of ministry.

1. Be prepared to spend time, not only in prep for your lessons and in prayer, but for home visitations. Parents often come to Christ through their children. (Is 11:6)
2. **Don't just <u>fill in</u>** because there's a plea for teachers. **<u>Fill up</u> each child's heart** with the truth in the Word of God, and demonstrate His love. Many in the Bible were young when they heard God's call. Teach your students to listen for His voice.
3. You may not be an evangelist, but you have the best avenue for the gospel to your children and their families. This is because **you have shown God's love and have a genuine point of contact.**
4. Plan to keep in touch with your kids and their families after they go on to the next class. Yes, your list of contacts will grow. You may need a whole team of assistants to help you keep up! Keep files and pass them on to the next teacher. You're part of a team! You are a blessing!

Father, being a teacher/leader of children is a huge responsibility. I'm trusting You for more grace, for favor, and anointing. Thank You, Lord.

Other passages for your prayerful consideration:
Dt 11:18-21; 1 Sm 16: 1-13; Ps 8:2, 78:1-7; Is 54:13; Jer 1:1-10; Mt 18:1-6; Lk 2:41-52 & 10:21; Acts 2:37-39; 1 Tm 4:12

Journaling: Think back to your spiritual gifts and personality assessments. Do you see anything that indicates that you'd make an effective teacher? Pray about entering this demanding, yet rewarding area of ministry.

Day Thirty-One:
Youth

Don't let anyone look down on you because you are young, but set an example for the believers in speech, in life, in love, in faith and in purity. (1 Tm 4:12)

"The things the Lord has done for my life have been endless. I was a typical 'stoner,' a slacker. I had no ambition for life, no drive, and basically felt like I had no purpose to live. The Lord lifted me up and today, I may not have as many friends, and I may not be as popular as I was, but I am the happiest I have ever been. I have a purpose; I have dreams; I have eternal life. Jesus Christ takes me higher than any drug ever could. The Lord has broken my chains. I am no longer bound. What started off as a fear of going to hell has now turned into a wonderful, amazing, eternal love for Jesus Christ. He takes me higher than any drug ever could!" (Jessie unknown)

I googled "Christian Teen Testimonies" and found Jessie's. It was fun reading them all, although some of the kids had a really hard time before coming to Christ. I didn't find my favorite story: "I accepted the Lord as my Savior when I was very young, before I got into a lot of trouble, and by His grace, I'm still His today." That's not the one we hear at revival meetings, but it's the best one anyone could have! Perhaps you're a young person reading this, or a parent of a teen. Maybe, you're even a youth pastor or worker. Whoever you are, my prayer is that this page will encourage you.

Personally, I was a wimpy Christian as a teen. I gave God a lot of lip service but never got grounded in His Word, never felt a need to repent of my sin, and had little prayer life. By the time I finished my teen years, I was completely backslidden. Actually, I don't think I was saved, even though I had prayed a sinner's prayer at a Christian camp at about age twelve. I finally hit bottom and turned to Jesus, asking Him to be my Lord at age twenty-six. My life really changed for the better, but **I've always regretted those missed years that I could have been serving Jesus.**

1. **Young person:** Hang in there. Get into (or stay in) the Word and let God speak into your life daily. Be faithful in the face of temptation, and hang with other kids who really love the Lord.
2. **Parent of a teen:** No matter where your son or daughter is with the Lord, serving Him or wandering, be diligent in your prayers. Keep giving of your time, and keep the lines of communication open. He or she may not act like it, but your teen needs you!
3. **Youth Pastor/Worker:** What can I say to you, Precious Servants, that you don't already know much better than I? I'm sure you're aware that in the next few years, your students will make the biggest decisions of their lives: "Can I really live for God and follow His standards as I go through life? . . . What kind of career will I have? . . . Do I need college for it? . . . What will I do with my life? . . . Will I marry? . . . How long will I remain single?"

A study done by The Barna Group (*Evangelism Is Most Effective among Kids*, October 11, 2004, www.barna.org) revealed that 77% of all decisions for Christ are made by age 21. I don't think there's a statistic for it, but I'll bet that a lot of the remaining 23% of those who make decisions are parents who come to Christ through their teens and the ministries of youth pastors and workers. **Want to be on the front lines, Christian worker? Hook up with your church's youth pastor.**

Jesus, you know what it's like to be a teen; You went through it! Thank You that You understand us from the inside out. Bless our youth, and if You choose, do so through me.

Other passages for your prayerful consideration:
Ps 37: 3-5; Prv 3: 1-35, 13:20, 21:30 & 27:6, 17

Journaling: Has God given you a heart for young people? They need people who are **relational** and **real**! If you have a Holy Spirit nudge towards youth, make a point of contacting the youth pastor in your community.

Day Thirty-Two:
Small Groups

They devoted themselves to the apostle's teaching and to the fellowship. . .They broke bread in their homes and ate together with glad and sincere hearts, praising God. . .and the Lord added to their number daily those who were being saved. (Acts 2: 42-47)

"You want to be baptized where?!?" Smitty lived in the "Playpen Apartments" where they had two pools, one for those who used suits and one for those who preferred none.

"We'll be able to wear our suits. I can reserve the pool," he assured us.

Getting baptized in that pool was an act of repentance for Smitty. The first night he came to the Campus Christian Fellowship, Smitty was well-dressed compared to the rest of us Jesus-hippies in the room, with slacks and a turtleneck sweater. He had tucked a huge family Bible with a picture of Jesus on the front under his arm. He kept coming and asked about being baptized. The gospel was explained simply and Smitty accepted Christ. He had a magnetic personality and was a one-man cheer leader for the University of Nevada, Las Vegas (UNLV). He would run around the stadium or basketball gym with a UNLV IS #1 sign in the air and big smile on his face. After accepting Christ and being baptized, he kept the same message on one side of his sign, but on the other it said, "JESUS IS #1!" Smitty would also hold up his sign at busy intersections in town. He was quite a sight in "Sin City" (Vegas). Jesus changed his life, and many came to know the Lord through him.

I don't think Smitty would have begun his Jesus journey from a pew. Norm and Sylvie's apartment was a lot less scary, which was true for many who came to know the Lord while attending our small group. My co-leader, Norm, and I taught; my wife, Dona, whom I met at that group, led worship. She and I have been involved with home groups/small groups ever since and have seen many lives touched with the gospel.

I love the above passage. The book of Acts highlights a lot of amazing events, but when you read this passage carefully, you will find one of the most exciting facts about the new church. **People were not coming to the Lord only through the apostles directly. People were being saved daily in homes! And it can be the same today.** Your neighbors could be a little shy about coming to church with you, but they may be willing to attend a small Bible study, perhaps with just two couples: you and your spouse, and them. Small groups provide a great place for Christians to grow in faith. Intimacy and accountability are easier for some than in a larger congregational setting.

Do you think all the home group leaders in the days of Acts had evangelism as a dominant gift? I doubt it. There were probably similar statistics then as now, and most believers had other gifts, **yet, . . .** *"The Lord added to their number daily those who were being saved."* (Acts 2:47) Not only is it easier in homes for people who don't yet know Jesus, it's easier for us. It's more natural to invite neighbors, friends at work, and others in our circles of influence to our homes than it is to ask them about attending church. After meeting for a while, they'll be more comfortable and perhaps start attending through a special event at church. Eventually, these precious ones will come to know Jesus!

Don't forget to pray for those in your circles of influence. **It's amazing how the Lord opens doors when we pave the way with prayer.** You don't need to be a Bible scholar to lead a group. Many tools are available to help you lead a discussion. I hope you'll prayerfully consider starting a group soon.

Father, You sent Your Son so that everyone would have an opportunity to be reconciled to You. Do You want me to start a small group in my home? Whom should I invite? Please pave the way.

Thank You, Lord.

Other passages for your prayerful consideration:
Acts 4:12-31; Rom 16:3-4; Col 4:15; Phlm 1:1, 2

Journaling: Look at the prayer above again, and answer the two questions. You may not sense a leading to start a group. Are you in one now? If not, consider joining one. You may learn to lead one by example.

Day Thirty-Three:
Christian Schools, Preschools, and Day Care

From the lips of children and infants You have ordained praise. (Ps 8:2; Mt 21:16)

"No one can do it like you, kids! If I sing, your parents may cry but for the wrong reason. You are going to touch hearts with this Christmas Program!" I lost track of the number of programs that I've been a part of in my thirty years in Christian Education, but I don't recall one where we didn't see people committing their hearts to the Lord! God opens doors, but He could do more with a plan.

Randy and Susan wanted the best education they could find for their little girl, Amy, and our school was a good fit for them. It wasn't long before one of Amy's new friends invited her to Missionettes on Wed. night. Amy's parents decided that rather than go clear home and back, they'd just sit in the back of the sanctuary during the Wednesday night service. One Sunday, a short time later, Dona and I met this humble young couple who had responded to the altar call at the end of the service. I'll never forget the sincere expressions on their faces as they committed their lives to Christ. I just spoke to Randy and Susan and asked for permission to share their story. As I write, they're celebrating seventeen years of pastoring at Sequim Four Square in Washington State!

I could tell you more amazing stories. I'm sure that's true for most of you who've ever been involved in Christian Education, yet I'm ashamed to confess that we weren't nearly as diligent as we should have been in fishing the ponds of Christian schools, preschools, and day care centers. **Reaching the families should be the most important motivation for having these ministries.** Here's a skeleton plan:

1. First, if there is a sponsoring church, the church community led by the pastors and boards, needs to **be committed to reaching out** to the school/preschool/ daycare families who have no home church or who may be involved in cults.
2. Second, the application for enrollment should include a place to indicate the regular place of worship. There can be a box for "none". The information needs to be organized: those who mark <u>none</u>, those in a cult, those who attend the sponsoring church, and those that have another home church already. This information helps to address evangelistic and other needs effectively.
3. About a month after school starts, teams of two can call on these families and ask how the school is doing with meeting the needs of their child(ren). Here are some guidelines for the conversation:
   a. What do you like best about the school?
   b. What is one area where we need improvement?
   c. From there, the team needs to be really sensitive to the Spirit's leading. People may be very open to the gospel. Sometimes, they are backslidden Christians. **There's no need to be pushy, but realize that you may have an opportunity to lead a family to Christ.**

    d.   You might have an open door to say, "We noticed that you don't have a church home. Would you be interested in more information about our church?"

    e.   Schedule a follow-up visit if appropriate.

Caution: In every school I've led, I've reminded the parents, "If it doesn't happen at home for kids, it's likely not to happen." The foundation of education and Christian faith is in the home. The Christian School Ministry offers support for the home. **A word to parents: no matter where your children are in school, be involved!** There are wonderful opportunities to share Christ in the public school arena, too. Many dedicated Christians are on the front lines there as educators, other staff, students, and parents.

Father, help us to be good stewards of the children and their families. Thank You, Lord.

Other passages for your prayerful consideration:
1Pe. 3:15; Eph 5:15-16; Col 4:5-6; Review the thoughts and passages from Day 22.

Journaling: Does your church have one or more of these ministries? Do your children attend a Christian school? How could you be involved in serving these families?

Day Thirty-Four:
Community Involvement

. . . Come, you who are blessed by my Father; take your inheritance,
the kingdom prepared for you since the creation of the world. For I
was hungry and you gave Me something to eat, I was thirsty and you
gave Me something to drink, I was a stranger and you invited Me in,
I needed clothes and you clothed Me, I was sick and you looked after
Me, I was a prisoner and you came to visit Me. . . . I tell you the truth,
whatever you did for the least of these brothers of Mine, you did it for
Me. (Mt 25:34-40)

Jim was a tall, lanky guy with the letters L-O-V-E tattooed on the knuckles of each hand. He was one of the many homeless that we served at the park. Once a month our church offered to our homeless friends meals, clothes, haircuts, a concert and testimonies. I greeted our guests saying, "Thank you all for sharing your day with us today. We know we're not doing enough, but we're grateful for the opportunity to do this little bit." We saw many lives turned around, but Jim was special. We were able to help him get work. He got on his feet, bought a motorcycle, and got an apartment. After he had started coming to church, he met a Christian girl, and they got married. They were very happy and went everywhere together on Jim's bike. After a while, they began to serve in various capacities. When they moved to another state, we had confidence that they would find a good church and continue growing in the Lord.

One of the great things about community involvement is that it allows us all to participate with our various gifts, personalities, and passions. If we share the message in words only, we've missed the call of the gospel. We need to be reaching, touching, and demonstrating the love of Jesus in our communities. Demonstration Gospel gives power to Word Gospel. As I write, the world is trying to climb out of the worst recession since the Great Depression of the 1930's. Governments are broke. We, the Church, gave away our responsibility for the poor, and NOW is our opportunity!

For many outside the faith, church is meaningless. "Oh yeah, if I want religion, I can get it there."

Community involvement makes us relevant:

"That's the church that serves a meal every week to the poor and homeless."

"That's the church that partnered with the city to. . ."

"That's the church that spent a Sunday morning helping people instead of having a service as usual."

There are so many ways to be relevant in your community. How do you start?

1. Like anything we do that's worthwhile, **we begin with prayer**. Involve as many people as possible. Pastor, you may need to set aside a Sunday morning service for just this purpose.

2. Follow prayer with a brainstorming session. **Do not worry about whether or not you can meet every need raised.** Ask God which need(s) He wants to meet through your church community.
3. Take an action step. Form a committee to look into the decided area(s) of need, and set a date to meet again. **Start small, but keep moving.**
4. Meet, listen, and get your "ducks in a row." **Set a date to start the ministry.**

Let's go back to Day 24. **Plan to look for opportunities to gently and respectfully share the gospel in words as you minister in the community.** Many groups and individuals do good deeds. We're different. **We are motivated by the love of God to share by meeting present <u>and</u> eternal needs.**

Jesus, Your mission is ours. Show us how we can touch people with the reality of Your love, for now and for eternity. Thank You, Lord.

Other passages for your prayerful consideration:
Ps 103:6, 107:8-16, 140:12, 146:7-9; Prv 14:21, 31, 19:17, 21:13, 22:9, 24:11-12; Is 58:6-12; Lk 4:18-19; Jas 1:27, 2:14-17; 1 Jn 3:16

Journaling: Does your church have special ways of reaching into your community? Are you involved? What are some other ways to reach out? Would there be a role that you could play in a new community ministry?

Day Thirty-Five:
Events: "the Byways" . . .

Jesus replied, "A certain man was preparing a great banquet and invited many guests. At the time of the banquet he sent his servant to tell those who had been invited, 'Come, for everything is now ready.' But they all alike began to make excuses. . . . The servant came back and reported this to his master. Then the owner of the house became angry and ordered his servant, 'Go out quickly into the streets and alleys of the town and bring in the poor, the crippled, the blind, and the lame.' 'Sir,' the servant said, 'what you ordered has been done, but there is still room.' Then the master told his servant, 'Go out to the roads and the country lanes and make them come in so that my house will be full.'" (Lu. 14:16-23)

"I feel awful!" Dona didn't look well.

"Well, we'd better take your temperature," I suggested. . . . "104! Wow!" "Do you think it could be an attack?" She asked.

"I don't know, Babe. Let's pray." It was Sunday afternoon, and the Christmas Program was that night. The choir was to sing from a huge tree that had been built, and Dona had the "altar call song." She still felt pretty bad, but we went to church. As we left the choir room to go into the sanctuary, Dona stuck her head out of a doorway and vomited. But she didn't give up. It had been decided that she would sit in a chair at the base of the tree until her song came up. When that time came, her voice was as beautiful as I've ever heard. Nineteen people responded to the invitation! Afterward, before we even went home, we found a thermometer. Her temperature was normal! It had been an attack.

What does this story tell you? One, **the enemy will fight your efforts to reach out with the gospel.** Two, God allows us to be tested so we learn to trust Him and grow stronger. Three, evangelistic events can be effective in drawing people to the Savior.

However, there is a downside to outreach through a special event. Friends, you'll find it in numerous studies that ask the question, "How effective are the various ways that Christians make the gospel known?" Evangelistic events are at or near the bottom. **People need more than a one-time experience of meeting Jesus as Savior. They need to know Him as Lord.** There are solutions.

1. After you take a friend to an event and they accept Christ, you can mentor them.
2. Altar workers (You will need many!) must be willing to make a new friend and help them grow into maturity. They need one-on-one time in the Word and in prayer.
3. As soon as possible, new believers need to be introduced to a small group and/or church.

The goal of discipleship is to help new believers come to the place where they are mature in their faith and are able to mentor someone themselves.

So, plan events. Participate in them. Events are not THE way to share the gospel, but they are A way. *"Come, follow me," Jesus said, "and I will make you fishers of men."* (Mt 4:19) Fishing is a science. A few days ago we watched a man pull in a four-foot shark while fishing off the Seal Beach pier. It was fascinating! People fish in ponds, streams, rivers, lakes, and oceans. They do it with poles, nets, and all kinds of other equipment. They fish from boats, at the edge of the water, and wading in the water. They're wise about bait, lures, the weight of the line, and types of poles and hooks. They fish differently depending on what type of fish they're trying to catch. Fishing requires skill and patience. **Fishing for souls demands God's help.** . . . *He who wins souls is wise.* (Prv 11:30)

Father, may Your gospel be like nectar to bees as we work in Your harvest field. Thank You.

Other passages for your prayerful consideration:
Mt 15:29-38; Jn 6:1-15; Acts 2:36-41, 4:1-4

Journaling: Does your church have special events? Are there wider efforts that your church supports? How might the Lord use you in this area?

Week 6

Cults, Other Religions, Hard Questions, Agnostics, and Atheists

Day Thirty-Six:
How Do I Talk with Mormons (Latter Day Saints - LDS)?

> *...Satan himself masquerades as an angel of light. It is not surprising, then, if his servants masquerade as servants of righteousness.* (2 Cor 11:14-15) *But even if we or an angel from heaven should preach a gospel other than the one we preached to you, let him be eternally condemned! As we have already said, so I say again: If anybody is preaching to you a gospel other than the one you have accepted, let him be eternally condemned.* (Gal 1:8-9)

"Emma, you're a good Christian Mormon lady, aren't you?" Emma was one of my Fuller Brush customers. She was a sweet older lady who had a big family Bible on her coffee table. I had just committed my life to Christ and was looking for a church. "Tell me about the Mormon church." Even though I liked her, what she told me just didn't ring true. I had the feeling that I had to be a Mormon to be really saved. God gave me discernment. I didn't say it aloud, but wondered, "Are Mormons real Christians?" The next day God, in His goodness, sent a Christian mailman, a friend from the past, by my house. He asked if I was in "fellowship" (I guessed he meant "church." Watch your use of "Christian-ese.") I told him I was kind of thinking of the Mormon Church.

"No, you don't wanna do that, Man." Ed got me into a good Bible believing, Jesus-and-people-loving church.

Dr. Walter Martin wrote a book awhile back called *The Maze of Mormonism*, and so it is. You could get lost in meaningless dialog. Don't! When you talk with a Mormon, **stick with three essential doctrines. If the foundation is wrong, the whole building is wrong.** They say that their foundation is Christ, but it's a different Jesus and a different gospel. Below, I will summarize the differences between Mormon and Christian doctrines on these three subjects and give a few verses of support.

Foundation One: The Nature of God

By definition, Bible Christianity is a monotheistic religion. **We believe in One Triune God: the Father, the Son, and the Holy Spirit.** Mormons believe in many gods; in fact, they believe that men can become gods. In the past, their prophets have even taught that the God we worship was once a man. **The Bible is clear. There is only one God, and He was never a man.** (Ex 8:10; Dt 4:35, 5:7, 6:4; Is 44:6, 8, 45:5-6, 14, 18, 21-22, 46:9; Mk 12:29; 1Cor 8:4-6; Eph 4:3-5; 1 Tm 2:5; Jas 2:19)

Foundation Two: The Nature of Christ

The Jesus of the Bible is the eternal Son of God. He always existed with the Father and the Holy Spirit. The Mormon Jesus is the spirit brother of Satan, pro-created in heaven by a father and mother god. On the surface, Mormonism looks like the Christian church down the street, but when you go a little deeper, you find the real differences between Christian and Mormon doctrine. [Gn 1:26. . . *God* (sing.) *said,* *"Let us. . ."* (plural); Is 9:6; Jn 1:1-5, 14, 10:30, 14:1-10; Col 1:15-20, 2:9; Heb 1:1-3]

Foundation Three: The Way of Salvation

In biblical Christianity, we receive righteousness *from* God through faith in Jesus; Mormons try to earn it through obedience to the organization's doctrines and practices. In Mormonism, your works earn you higher levels of salvation, the ultimate being godhood **A Christian's works flow naturally out of relationship with God the Father, through God the Son, by the power of the indwelling Holy Spirit**.. (Jn 1:12-13, 3:3-8, 16-17, 6:28-29, 10:27-28, 14:1-6; Acts 16:29-34; Rom1:17, 3:19-26, 6:23, 10:9-13, 2 Cor 5:17, 21; Eph 2:1-10; Phil 1:6; Col 3:1-4; Ti 3:5-7; 1 Pt 1:18-19; 1 Jn 5:11-13)

Lord, may there be a groundswell – a revelation of Your truth in the LDS organization. Thank You for Your truth!

Journaling: Is anyone in your "Oikos" a Mormon? Pray for an opportunity to share the true biblical gospel.

Day Thirty-Seven:
What if the Jehovah's Witnesses (JWs) Come Knocking?

They are. . .always learning but never able to acknowledge the truth.
(2 Tm 3:6-7)

"I'm sure that everything you're telling me is true. You're very nice, and you're quoting from the Bible. There's just one thing that perplexes me. I just accepted Jesus into my heart last night, and He has filled me with an incredible joy! Forgive me for saying so, but you don't seem to be very joyful." The next day, one of the two women returned and knocked on the door. "Oh, you came back! Alone?"

The girl replied that she was being trained, and that she was actually pretty new to JWs. "I got to thinking about your comment. You're right. I don't have joy. I just had to come back. I need God's joy. How do I get it?"

"Well, let me share what happened to me. Jesus will do the same for you." So a new disciple won another!

Jehovah's Witnesses is another religion that looks a lot like biblical Christianity, but you don't have to look very far to see their heresy. They have the four marks that all cults have:

1. **All cults have a human leader who must also be believed in order to gain full salvation.** With Mormons, it's Joseph Smith. Jehovah's Witnesses have the Watchtower Society.
2. **All cults distort the deity of Jesus Christ.** With Mormons, he's the spirit brother of Satan. JWs teach that Jesus was created, not eternal, formerly existing as the archangel, Michael.
3. **All cults bend Scripture.** They either write their own in addition to the Bible, as the LDS organization does, or like JWs; they alter the translations to fit their own doctrines.
4. **All cults require works for ultimate salvation.** This leads to self-righteousness rather than righteousness **from** God on the basis of humble faith in Jesus. (Mt 6:22-23) In both Mormonism and Jehovah's Witnesses, you must be baptized into their organization, the "only true church."

It's not every day that someone comes to your door wanting to talk about God. Jehovah's Witnesses and Mormon "elders" do. **Keep the conversation centered**

on essential Bible based doctrine. Following are some examples of where JWs err regarding the nature of Christ. Use these to plant seeds of doubt in their false religion:

1. **Jn 1:1** - Most Christian Bibles - *In the beginning was the Word, and the Word was God*. The New World (Jehovah Witness) Translation – ". . . the Word was <u>a god</u>." They ask a lot of questions. Here's a good one for them: If Jesus was "a god", wouldn't that make Him an idol? We're only supposed to worship God, but the wise men came to worship Jesus (Mt 2:1-2) and Joseph and Mary let them (vs.11). He Himself received worship from his disciples in Mt 14:33 and Lk 24:52, by the women in Mt 28:17, and by Thomas in Jn 20:28. **Jesus never demanded worship, but He received it** again from the blind man in Jn 9:38. Heb 1:6 tells us that angels worship Him.

2. **Col 1:15-20** – When you look up this passage, you will see clearly that Jesus was the Creator (as was the Father and the Holy Spirit). But in the New World Translation (NWT), the word "other" is inserted three times, which is why it's in brackets: "by means of him all [other] things were created. . .All [other] things have been created through him and for him. . .and by means of him all [other] things were made to exist." (Westcott and Hort 1969) This **one added word makes Jesus a created being instead of the eternal Creator**. (Their *Kingdom Interlinear Translation of the Greek Scriptures*, with Greek and the NWT side by side shows this clearly. The Watchtower Society no longer publishes this, but you can get it on the internet.)

3. **Rom 10:13 compared to Phil 2:11** – This point centers around the translation of the Greek word for "Lord". JWs generally translate the word "Jehovah". In the NWT, the Romans passage says, "Everyone who calls on the name of **Jehovah** (not "Lord") will be saved. In Phil the Greek is translated "Lord," not "Jehovah." With the same translation method, it would read, ". . .Jesus Christ is **Jehovah** to the glory of God the Father." To JWs, that would be the same as saying that Jesus is God.

Father, thanks that I can share what the Bible clearly teaches about You, Jesus, and salvation

Journaling: The next time JWs come knocking at your door, will you send them away or not answer? What can you do to be prepared to *give an answer*? (1 Pt 3:15)

Day Thirty-Eight:
How Can I Share My Faith with Muslim Friends?

*I write these things . . . that you may **know** that you have eternal life.*
(1 Jn 5:13)

Zinah worked in the same office as Sarah, and they shared a break together one day. As they talked, Zinah revealed that she was in the process of immigrating to the United States from Iraq. Sarah was genuinely interested in her new friend. "I love your name, Zinah. What does it mean?"

"My parents are Muslim," she replied. "It's a family name meaning 'Beauty.' What does Sarah mean?"

Sarah chuckled. "It means 'Princess.' We should put our names together – Beautiful Princess!"

Zinah laughed too. "Sarah, can I ask you something?" Sarah nodded. "Are you a Christian?"

Smiling, Sarah replied, "Yes, I am. I hope that's OK."

"O yes," Zinah assured her, "actually, I'm very interested in Christianity. In my country, we are not allowed to associate with Christians, but now that I'm here, I'd like to know what you believe."

"Well, sure, I'd love to learn more about Islam, too."

You may find that people who practice Islam here and those who emigrate from Muslim countries are very interested in Christianity. They understand it as a religion and may have no clue that it entails a relationship with God through Jesus. **When sharing your faith with a Muslim, as with anyone really, developing a relationship is very important.** The little story above displays the beginning of a relationship that could include an ongoing discussion about faith. Let's address some concerns that Zinah might have.

1. Sarah may not need to give evidence that the Bible is trustworthy, but if she does, the religious book for Muslims, **the Qur'an, holds a key for establishing the Bible as reliable.** Muslims are taught that the Bible has been corrupted. However, many passages in the Qur'an uphold the Bible as a book to be not only trusted, but revered. (See the Qur'an, Sura: V.71, VI.115) The Qur'an was written by Mohammed, who Muslims consider to be the true prophet. According to Mohammed, the angel Gabriel gave him the revelation in AD 610. The Dead Sea Scrolls, which contain copies of scripture that date back over 1000 years before the time of Mohammad, prove that today's Bible translations are accurate, which would make corruption impossible. If they were, the Qur'an itself would be tainted. (Schlemon 2010)

2. Zinah might be even more willing to hear Sarah out if she knows some basic beliefs of Islam: "God" in Arabic is "Allah." They believe in good and bad angels and in life after death. They believe that Ishmael, not Isaac, was the child of promise. (Read Gn 15 and 16.) While Mohammed is the founder

of their religion, they believe Abraham, Moses, David, and even Jesus were true prophets. **They believe a lot about Jesus but not that He died on the cross for our sins and rose again.** This is why you may need to establish the authority of the Bible. They also believe that Jesus will return to earth and declare Islam as the true religion. Muslims do not believe in salvation by grace through faith. There are works that they must do, and if their good works do not outweigh the bad, they go to hell. The works include their confession: "There is no God but Allah and Mohammed is the prophet of God," prayer five times a day, giving alms, fasting during Ramadan, and making a pilgrimage to Mecca. **There's no assurance of salvation.**

3. Zinah may have a "Hollywood" view of Christianity, so establishing a friendship is crucial. **Your personal story, blended with the true story of Jesus, is very important.** Sarah would want to be respectful of the culture and try to answer questions. She should be ready to share the biblical basis for salvation. It would be very good news to Zinah that she could *know* she is accepted and loved by God and would definitely spend eternity in heaven!

Lord, as the world of Islam opens up more and more, You may give me an opportunity to share the Gospel with a person who has a Muslim background. Thank you for Your guidance.

Other passages for your prayerful consideration:
Rom 12:9; Review passages from Day 23

Journaling: Islam is the fastest growing religion in the world. Your Jesus story could positively impact a Muslim friend. Practice telling it again.

Day Thirty-Nine:
What Do I Need to Know about Eastern Religions:
Hinduism, Buddhism. . .?

. . .You will know the truth, and the truth will set you free. (Jn 8:32)

"I've heard that saying before," Mrs. Singh said looking at the back of her receipt. She had just ordered some Fuller Brush products from me. I'd had a stamp made of John 3:16. "It's actually a quote from the Bible," I informed her.

"Ah, the Bible," she replied. As we talked, Mrs. Singh shared with me that she believed in reincarnation. I explained that Jesus offered something better than another life here; He offered eternal life in Paradise.

"Ah, eventually," she concurred, "but it's a long journey that may require many lives. You believe that God lives inside you, right?" she asked.

"Yes, I do," I replied simply.

"So do I," she said. Then she quoted Scripture. *"In my Father's house are many mansions."* (Jn 14:2)

She had me! I walked right into her trap. If I hadn't been so sure of myself, I would have shown her the context of that passage (Jn 14:1-6) and how Jesus promised to return for us and that the only way to the Father was through Him. But, I was too rattled. I blew it. That was many years ago when I was better at talking than listening and thoughtfully responding!

Because there are so many eastern religions, in this short space I'll share in generalities. A belief in reincarnation is common to many eastern religions. Other non-scriptural beliefs include polytheism (many gods - good and bad, creative and destructive), and ancestor worship. Confucianism and Buddhism are described as "ways of life" rather than religions. Another common belief in Hinduism and its many offshoots, such as Transcendental Meditation, is that god is in all, and everything is god. **When God gives you opportunity to share with any religion with which you are unfamiliar, there are two main rules of conduct: 1. Know what you believe, especially about Jesus. Most of these religions at least respect Him as a divine**

teacher. 2. Listen well and respectfully, and do your homework. Following, I will address some common beliefs and contrast them with Christian faith.

1. **Reincarnation** is related to something that many eastern religions call "Karma." The scriptural counterpart would be "you reap what you sow." Karma teaches that you are rewarded or punished in this life for your deeds in your previous life. You go through this process until you reach god-consciousness. Heb 9:27 says, *". . .man is destined to die once, and after that to face judgment. . . ."* Sin and forgiveness receive little attention in religions that believe in reincarnation because sin is <u>paid for</u> by Karma, and good deeds are rewarded.
2. **Polytheism** is the belief in many gods. Many actions and worship are centered on appeasing one or more of these gods. **The Bible declares throughout that there is but One True Eternal God Who manifests Himself as Father, Son, and Holy Spirit.** (Mk 12:29-31) While God comes to abide in Christians at salvation, we do not become gods, nor are we part of God.
3. **Ancestor worship** occurs in ancient cultures all over the world, even in modern times. It is founded on the belief that the dead are able to influence lives in later generations. These ancestors can assert their powers by blessing or cursing, and so their worship is inspired by both respect and fear. Many, especially those embracing Shintoism, still practice this religion.

Father, these eastern religions are confusing! If You open the door for me to share my faith with someone who adheres to one, I trust that You will help me to respond respectfully, and explain Your truth convincingly. Thank You for Your simple gospel.

Other passages for your prayerful consideration:
Prv 12:17, 19, 14:5; Jn 3:31-36, 8:31-32, 14:1-9

Journaling: Do you know anyone that adheres to an Eastern religion? Write a sentence or two telling how your Jesus story could be a positive influence.

Days Forty & Forty-One:
How Do I Answer Hard Questions?

CHALLENGES TO OUR FAITH MAY COME FROM WITHIN OR FROM OTHERS. WE WILL BRIEFLY ADDRESS THREE "HARD QUESTIONS." OF COURSE, THERE ARE MORE. PREPARE YOURSELF BY SEARCHING OUT THESE MATTERS WITH THE LORD. WE MAY CONCLUDE THAT WE DON'T UNDERSTAND, BUT THAT WE SIMPLY TRUST GOD AND HIS CHARACTER.

1. Why does God allow suffering?

Pharaoh asked Jacob, "How old are you?" And Jacob said to Pharaoh, "The years of my pilgrimage are a hundred and thirty. My years have been few and difficult. . . ." (Gen. 47:8-10)

"If there is a god, and if he is good, then he would want to prevent his creatures from suffering. If he were almighty, he could do what he wanted. Therefore, he either is not good, or he is not all-powerful, or he doesn't exist at all!"

John was stunned by the anger in his challenger's face and voice. Remaining calm, he replied gently with respect. "Sir, could you be misplacing the blame for suffering onto God? He created us with free will. We've abused that gift by ignoring His moral law and hurting one another."

The man sneered! "Is it my choice that women and children are starving to death in Sudan?"

John replied, "Sir, we all have rebelled against God. The Bible calls that sin. We are not only all sinners, but we all are also victims of sin. God wants to redeem the whole world. That's why He sent His Son. But we must freely choose Him. A love relationship cannot exist without choice." The challenger's face softened. John continued, "God has made the choice to love us in spite of our sin, but He won't force us to accept Him."

The man's voice was much quieter. "I still don't understand why God would allow horrible suffering."

John replied, "If it hurts our hearts to see the misery people endure, think of how it hurts the great heart of God! God desires a relationship with each of us. I don't fully understand it, but I think that, to God, you and I were worth His pain due to rejection by some, and the anguish that it's caused." There was no reply, but John did not try to "close the deal." "Would you think about what I've shared with you? Can we talk some more later?"

The man nodded, "I guess so."

Before they exchanged phone numbers, John asked, "Do you own a Bible?"

The man didn't look up, but he nodded, "Yes." He chuckled. "I think I can find it."

"May I suggest that you read the Gospel of John? It will put you in touch with God's heart."

The story above is taken from bits and pieces of actual conversations, although, unfortunately, many did not end as well. **Sometimes these "hard questions" are**

really excuses for not wanting to face a holy God in our sinfulness, but other times they are asked honestly. These questions may actually be saying, "If I were God. . . ." In our sin, each of us would be our own god. **Because we identify with these people, we have an opportunity.**

Other passages for your prayerful consideration:
Is. 52:13-53:12; Ezr 18:1-32; Rom 8:16-28; Heb 11:1-12:3

2.   How could a God of love send anyone to hell?

> *The rich man . . . answered, "Then I beg you father (Abraham) send Lazarus to my father's house, for I have five brothers. Let him warn them, so that they will not also come to this place of torment."*
> (Lu. 16:19-31)

Norman's family stood around his hospital bed and watched the heart monitor. Suddenly, there was the flat line. His wife let out a little whimper. His two daughters began to weep. His oldest son smacked his right fist into his left palm. Jimmy, the youngest boy looked down, his hands folded in front of him. Only a few seconds had passed by when one of the daughters gasped, "Look!" She was pointing to her father's face. "His eyelids flickered! There they go again! Did you see that?" The heart monitor had come to life. Norman's eyes opened. He sat up with a look of horror on his face. He glanced quickly at each family member, all with their mouths wide open.

"Norman?" his wife said softly. Norman felt himself as though he was checking to make sure he was really alive. "Sweetheart, we're all here." A doctor rushed into the room followed by two nurses. They checked and rechecked. The man was completely well! They walked out shaking their heads.

Norman's family gathered around. "Jimmy, we need to talk. I just caught a glimpse of hell, and I think I met your Jesus. He pulled me back! Son, will ya help me pray right now?"

The young man smiled broadly. "Right now is great, Dad." The whole family bowed their heads and repeated the prayer that Jimmy prayed, and all of their lives were forever changed.

There are many ideas about hell. The Bible says it was made *for the devil and his angels.* (Mt 25:41) Hell is a place from which God has simply withdrawn His presence. Sin separates people from a holy God and cannot exist in His presence. Sadly, **some choose not to turn from sin.** Consider this thought: Hell is a reflection of God's wisdom and mercy. Sound strange? If the end is simply death, what is there to deter us from doing even more harm to one another? I don't understand everything about God. One day faith will become sight.

Other passages for your prayerful consideration:
Mt 25:31-46, Jn 3:16-21, 36; Rom 2:5-16, 3:21-28

3. Why Did God, in the Old Testament, command the annihilation of women and children?

When God saw what they (the people of Nineveh) *did and how they turned from their evil ways, He had compassion and did not bring on them the destruction He had threatened.* (Jon 3:10)

" I s that the only possible option?" It had been a horrible accident. They said Jason was lucky to have survived the fall and even more so to be found before dying from exposure. He had fallen while hiking and compound fractures in both legs left him immobile. When he was discovered after three days, he was unconscious, but alive. Gangrene had set into both legs. Antibiotics had been ineffective. Without amputation Jason would die.

"At this point, it is our only option if we are to save him," the surgeon grimly replied. Jason's parents were horrified, but they gave the go-ahead the doctor needed. Jason lost his legs, but his life was spared.

The violence of the Old Testament is difficult to read. Such was war in ancient times. It's not much more humane today. In the Old Testament, it is clear that God gave specific orders for entire nations to be wiped out including women, children, and even beasts. **"How could this have been the judgment of a loving God?"**

A common conclusion is that He wouldn't judge in this way and therefore, "The Old Testament is not reliable, so how can the words of the New Testament, with salvation's Savior and message, be trusted?" Perhaps you've asked this question yourself. I also have wrestled with this. **The Old Testament has an overall theme: "God is holy; Man is sinful." (The New Testament picks it up, and its message is, "Man is hopelessly sinful, but God has provided a remedy for our reconciliation to Himself.")** When the time came to bring judgment on the Canaanite nations, Israel was commanded to . . .*not leave alive anything that breathes. . .otherwise, they will teach you to follow the detestable things they do in worshipping their gods, and you will sin against the Lord, your God.* (Dt 20:16-18) But, Israel did not obey God. The "gangrene" was not cut out. **Israel was judged just like the other nations because of unrepentant sin and idolatry** which included sacrificing children by fire, temple prostitution, sodomy, and bestiality. (Lv 18:21-30) But, the question remains, "Why the children?" This seems hard, but consider the alternative. Would they have grown up bitter and committed the same heinous sins as their parents? **Did God, in His mercy, take the children in their innocence to be with Him in heaven?**

God's judgment in the OT was harsh, but the redemption of mankind came with an even more severe penalty, the torture and crucifixion of His sinless Son, Jesus Christ. **His cross depicts in its two beams the judgment and the love of God meeting.** His justice had to be satisfied even as His love, mercy, and grace were extended.

Father, Thank You that it's okay to ask hard questions. Help me to trust Your impeccable character.

Other passages for your prayerful consideration:
Is 1:16-20, 55:8-9; Heb 11:1, 6; 1 Pt 1:15-21

Journaling: Maybe you've faced tough questions and just moved on. If not, I encourage you to keep a separate "Hard Questions" Journal. If someone asks one, remember that it's okay to say, "I don't have all the answers."

Day Forty-Two:
How Do I Talk with Agnostics and Atheists?

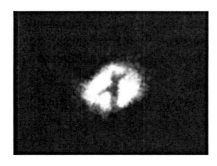

For since in the wisdom of God the world through its wisdom did not know Him, God was pleased through the foolishness of what was preached to save those who believe. (1 Cor 1:21)

Every day I passed him on my morning walk around the "island" that contains the mobile home park where we live. We greeted each other with smiles and friendly greetings. One morning I introduced myself.

"My name is Dominic," he replied, extending his hand. "I noticed that you pick up trash as you walk."

"Yeah, I do. It started here," I said glancing towards the church which was in the same "island."

"Why do you do that, if I may ask?" he inquired.

"Well, this is our home church, so I just clean up a little bit. One day I thought, 'this is my neighborhood' so I expanded my work."

"Oh, I'm not religious. I'm an atheist." A bit of a scowl crossed his face. As we talked, Dominic became angry. I wasn't sure why. I was careful to be polite and respectful as we conversed. When our paths crossed afterwards, he wouldn't return my greetings.

One day, I found pages torn from a Bible strewn all along my walking path. My heart broke, thinking it very well may have been Dominic. Our walk times aren't the same any more, but I occasionally pass by his mobile home or see him drive by. He still ignores my waves and I still pray for Dominic.

How do you witness for Christ to an atheist or an agnostic? Search the web, but plan on spending a lot of time. **There are many conversion testimonies.** This is only an introduction. Let me start with definitions:

- Atheism is the belief that there is no God. Therefore, there is no duty to God.
- Agnosticism is the belief that nothing is known or can be known about the existence of God.

These positions are also intertwined. Some call themselves "agnostic atheists," and some others "agnostic theists" who say that there may be a God. **Others personally use the tags but are really just running from God.**

You can tell by my story that I haven't had much success talking with these people, but I'll pass on what I'm learning from others. You'll also find some good resources in the appendix in the back.

1. **Be relational.** Know your atheist/agnostic. Let them fully express why they believe as they do. Ask questions: "What do you mean by 'God'"? "What kind of 'God' do you reject?" "What kind of evidence that 'God' exists would be acceptable to you?" While no one can gather test-tube proof of God's existence, experiential proof is hard to counter. **Share your own story** of how you came to faith in Christ. Include the emotions you felt and feel about the Lord. This may pique interest. **Pray.** (Jn 6: 44)
2. Ask the person how they believe the universe was formed, and **put your dogma on a leash,** for instance, in regard to creation versus evolution. Recent studies in genetics have given more scientific support for evolution, but the origin of the universe and of life are still scientific mysteries. **An atheist or agnostic need not give up his or her knowledge of science to accept that a supreme being exists.**
3. Raise the question of morality, our sense of right and wrong. It is true that much of this comes from how we are raised, but **there is also evidence that we are born with it.** Very tiny babies exhibit the exercise of free will and a sense of right and wrong.
4. **Don't be afraid to present the stories of the Bible and the words of Jesus Christ expressing forgiveness and love.** An atheist or agnostic may not give much credence to the Bible, but there is much evidence of its accuracy and reliability. One is fulfilled prophecy.
5. **Invite** your friend to church or a Christian event. **Remember, the Holy Spirit is your partner! Pray.**

Father, I know you exist because You've given me the gift of faith and we are in relationship. But I was once separated from you. Please open hard hearts to receive your grace and love.

Other passages for your prayerful consideration:
Ps 10:4, 14:1, 19:1-6, 36:1; Rom 1:18-20; 1 Cor 1:18-25

Journaling: Are you in contact with atheists or agnostics? If so, write down their names and pray for them. Do some research; equip yourself, and be ready to share your faith when God opens the doors.

Week 7

Walking with a New Believer
to Maturity in Christ

Day Forty-Three:
Discipleship: How Do I Help a New Christian to Grow?

Then Jesus came to them and said, "All authority in heaven and on earth has been given to Me.]Therefore, go and make disciples of all nations, baptizing them in the Name of the Father, and of the Son, and of the Holy Spirit, and teaching them to obey everything I have commanded you. And surely I am with you always, to the very end of the age." (The Great Commission: Mt 28:18-20)

Ted ran ahead to open the door for his wife, Dora, and their new baby girl, Tiffany. She went in and sat on the sofa. Her face was sad. Ted sat next to her. "What's the matter, Babe?"

"I don't know how to take care of her." Dora really seemed worried.

"Well, how hard can it be? I mean, she's just a baby." Ted almost seemed nonchalant, and that really got to his wife.

"Exactly!" she exclaimed. "I don't know how to be a mom! And you, obviously, know nothing about it!"

Rather than get angry, Ted wisely let it go. "Listen," he said, "I already went shopping and got everything Tiffany needs. I've got formula, diapers, clothes, everything!"

"You did?" Dora brightened. "Doesn't she look beautiful, just sleeping in my arms?"

Ted replied, "She sure does. And, Dora, her room is all ready too. Why don't we just let her lie her in her crib for now?" Ted took the sleeping beauty, and Dora followed them into the baby's room. He gently laid her down. "Wait here," he said. "I'll be right back!" In just a moment, Ted returned with his hands full of bags, and he set them at the end of the crib, opposite of where little Tiffany lay. "There," he said proudly, "Tiffany's got everything she needs. Now, stop worrying, OK?"

Dora glanced back over her shoulder with an unsure expression on her face as they left the baby. "That can't be all there is to it," she thought.

"Don't worry," Ted assured her, "Our baby has everything she needs right there in her crib!"

As silly as that story sounds, it portrays exactly what we often imply with new believers. "We serve meals at the church on Wednesday night, Sunday morning, and Sunday night. Want to grow? Show up." Some of you are thinking, "Yeah, that's how I came along." **Others of you were blessed with someone who really stuck close**

until you were grounded in the Lord. New believers need a lot of personal care, just like a baby. They need a spiritual "parent" – a friend. Jesus said. *"Come, follow Me. . ."* not "follow this plan." (Mt 4:19)

To help someone grow, we must be humble and growing ourselves, and one gateway for input is from the person we're mentoring. I had an unofficial discipling relationship with a young man named Dan. One day, I was complaining to him about how much work our new home was requiring. My attitude was not good. God set me straight when my friend said, "Well, Dave, I guess you guys needed the house, and the house needed you." Through Dan, God gave wise counsel and my whole perspective became more positive.

What do you do when sin enters your life and your new believer is aware of it? The temptation is to secure our high position in their minds by justifying and rationalizing, when what's needed is a demonstration of how to repent. **New Christians need to learn to practice 1 Jn 1:5-2:2: walking in the Light—confessing sin, and receiving forgiveness and cleansing by faith as a life-style.** What better way to learn it than by observation? Phariseeism has no place in a mentoring relationship. **Being a discipler means being an honest, godly friend.**

Lord, thank you for the opportunity to help someone progress into maturity in their walk with You. Please cause us to grow together in the knowledge of Christ.

Other passages for your prayerful consideration:
Phil 1:6-11, 3:7-17; 1 Tm 4:12; 1 Jn 1:5-2:2

Journaling: At some point in your life, you will be a mentor if you're not already. Write about how others have helped you to grow. You can do the same things. You are leading. Someone is following. Be purposeful.

Day Forty-Four:
Teaching My Friend How God "Speaks"

. . . His sheep follow Him because they know His voice. But they will never follow a stranger; in fact they will run away from him because they do not recognize a stranger's voice. (Jn 10:4-5)

"Hilda, my daughter," came the booming voice from above. Hilda, a retired missionary who had served for over fifty years in India, was tending the garden. "Who's there?" She called out, looking up.

Snickering in an office above the garden were the youth and senior pastors of the church. As soon as they could control themselves, the senior (yes, senior) pastor called again in the deepest voice he could muster, "Hilda, this is God!" The two pranksters hid themselves, but this time, they got no response. Soon, there was a knock at the pastor's door. With a straight face, Pastor answered, "Why, hello Hilda. Is something the matter?"

"Pastor," she replied, "I think you'd better have someone check the grounds. I heard a strange voice. It said it was God, but it wasn't. I <u>know</u> God's voice!"

So, the joke was on the pastors!

New Christians need to learn to know God's voice. Many times they're confused when they hear others say, "God spoke to me." "You mean, out loud?" they may ask. Elijah heard God's voice as a whisper. (1 Kgs 19:9-18) *. . .Your ears will hear a voice behind you saying, "This is the way; walk in it."* (Is 30:21) I have heard God's voice. **Usually, He speaks to me through His Word.** As I read, study, meditate on, and memorize Scripture, I take time to be silent before the Lord, listening for the impressions He will put on my heart. There have been times when I'm just reading along, and a passage will leap off the page. **We need to learn to pause and listen** at these times.

Encourage your new follower of Jesus to keep a journal. **When those God thoughts come, they should be jotted down,** as well as prayers and answers to prayer. I once heard about a pastor who was praying in the sanctuary, at the altar. Suddenly, his mind was filled with a revelation from the Lord. He began to spontaneously praise and worship God, but when he finished, he forgot what he'd heard.

God speaks into our spirits, just as He speaks through His Word. **He can also speak through another person** – that could even be you. As a teacher of children, God spoke to me many times through them. **He can use a sermon or a song.** And sometimes, His voice comes from a completely unexpected source. **The issue is not whether or not God speaks. It's whether or not we're listening.**

Where does God live? He lives in our hearts. *If anyone loves Me, he will obey My teaching. My Father will love him, and <u>we</u> will come and make our home with him.* (Jn 14:23) How does that happen? Jesus didn't physically come into our hearts when we invited Him. The Holy Spirit entered our hearts at salvation and brought with Him the Father and the Son. **The triune God lives inside of every fully devoted follower of Jesus Christ! So, we need to be listening, expecting to hear His voice.**

I encourage you to meet with your mentee once a week for Bible study and prayer. At these times, you can be a model. You can encourage the new believer by discussing what they are "hearing" when they read and pray, and affirming them. He/she will grow in confidence on the road to maturity and become a mentor too. **That's the goal: disciples making disciples. . . making disciples . . . .**

Father, I want to hear Your voice. As You're teaching me to listen, help me to be a model so _____(your mentee's name) can learn to listen too. Thank You for speaking to us, Your children.

Other passages for your prayerful consideration:
Is 30:21; Rv 2:7, 11, 17, 29, 3:6, 13, 19-22

Journaling: Think and write about times when you've heard God's voice. What medium did He use?

Day Forty-Five:
Learning to Serve a 24/7 God, 24/7

O Lord. . .You know when I sit and when I rise. . .You are familiar with all my ways. . . . Where can I go from Your Spirit? . . . Your hand will guide me; Your right hand will hold me fast. . . . All the days ordained for me were written in Your book before one of them came to be. . . . I am (always) with You. (Ps 139:1-18)

"I was out making calls. It was snowing and cold. My heater wasn't working. The road was icy. The hill I was headed down went right by an old church. Rather than destroy the stone steps, they just paved the road around them. Suddenly, my car stalled and the brakes froze up. I was sliding and gaining speed fast, headed right for those steps. I closed my eyes just before impact and called out, 'Jesus!' When I opened my eyes, I was on the other side of the steps at the bottom of the hill. The car was running, and there was a warm glow inside." (told by Brother Brewer, best as I can remember)

Do you recall the fiery furnace story in Daniel, chapter 3? The people were ordered to worship the king's idol at the trumpet's sound. Only three heads remained up after the powerful blast. Do you remember what they said to the king when threatened? *"O Nebuchadnezzar. . .if we are thrown into the furnace, the God we serve is able to save us from it. . .but even if He does not, we will not serve your gods or worship the image of gold you have set up."* (Dn 3:16-18) The king was so angry, he had the furnace heated up seven times hotter than usual. The soldiers who threw Shadrach, Meshach, Abednego in, were burned up! When the king looked, he saw a fourth man! He was astonished! When the three came out, they didn't even smell like smoke. Not a hair on their bodies was singed. The king then commanded that everyone worship the one true God of the Hebrews.

There are many stories about God's faithful presence. You know some, too. **He promised He would never leave or forsake us.** (Heb 13:5-6) My daily prayer is, "Lord, help me to be <u>aware</u> of Your presence." It's so easy to get caught up in the busy-ness of the day. **We need to model awareness of the Lord's faithful presence with our new believer.** But we need to have balance. There are times when heaven seems closed. Some are not healed or delivered. What do we say about this reality? **I love Bible facts** when my emotions or difficult circumstances deceive me, and I can't understand or <u>feel</u> Him. Jesus loves me! He promised to never leave me! (Heb 13:5-6) **We need to help our mentees to rely on the Word, especially when our natural minds can't make sense of things.**

You take in food daily. Eat the Living Bread every day. You drink water daily. Drink the Living Water continually. **Jesus is the Bread of Life and the Living Water.** (Jn 6:35, 7:37-38) **Feed on the Word in your heart and fellowship with the Lord all day long.** I remember the first time I read, *Pray without ceasing.* (1 Thes 5:17) I thought, "I can do that? Cool!"

God promises His presence. Sometimes, He will deliver us; other times He will not answer our prayers the way we want Him to. Read Hebrews, chapter eleven. Read the history of Christians. Read Foxe's Book of Martyrs. Read today's news; there are more believers being martyred today than ever before in history. Don't buy the "health and wealth" false gospel. If the gospel cannot be proclaimed in the impoverished nations, it's not the gospel! But **never doubt the promise of His Presence!** Aren't you glad He's not available only on Sunday? Model living in the light 24/7, for we serve a 24/7 God.

Father, please continually draw me to You and Your Word. You promised to be with me always. Thank You that You are! Help me to live in the awareness of this fact.

Other passages for your prayerful consideration:
Ps 51:10-13; Mt 28:18-20; Jn 14:15-18

Journaling: Do you have any disciplines that help you to be more aware of God's presence? Write down what they are or could be. Put them into practice and share them with your mentee.

Day Forty-Six:
How Can I Nurture this New Relationship in Christ?

When he (Paul) *came to Jerusalem, he tried to join the disciples, but they were all afraid of him, not believing that he was really a disciple. But Barnabas took him and brought him to the apostles. He* (Barnabas) *told them* . . . (Saul/Paul's testimony) (Acts 9:26-28)

The mountains were spectacular! This time alone with God and my friend, Jimmy Stewart (not the movie star, but probably more famous in God's eyes), was priceless. We had history, my dear brother and I. We had like passion and calling. Jimmy's call had led him with his young family to Hong Kong, and face-to-face visits were (and still are) few and far in between. I was grateful that he could give me a day. We hiked, shared and laughed all day. Finally, we stopped in a beautiful quiet place to do what we really came to do - pray together. Afterward, we talked about what we felt the Lord was saying to us as individuals, and for one another. In all humility, Jimmy said, "Dave, you need to put yourself on the backside of the cross." I was committed to the Lord, but He wanted me to go to a deeper level, and God used my trusted friend to help me do so. I love him and he loves me; we have earned each other's respect. Jimmy is still ministering "The Father's Love" all over the Far East, and he's very busy. I still cherish our times together and look forward to more in the future.

"Jacob was a cheater, Peter had a temper, David had an affair, Noah got drunk, Jonah ran from God, Paul was a murderer, Gideon was insecure, Miriam was a gossiper, Martha was a worrier, Thomas was a doubter, Sarah was impatient, Elijah was moody, Moses stuttered, Zaccheus was short, Abraham was old, and Lazarus was dead. . . . **God doesn't call the qualified, He qualifies the CALLED!**" (anonymous) Like you, your mentee is called. Jacob had his wives, Peter had Andrew, David had Jonathan, Noah had his wife, Jonah had a fish, Paul had Barnabas, Gideon had an angel, Miriam had Moses, Martha had Mary, Thomas had the other apostles, Sarah had Abraham, Elijah had Elisha, Moses had Aaron; perhaps Zaccheus had Matthew (they were both tax collectors), Abraham had Sarah, Lazarus had his sisters and his best friend, Jesus! **Your mentee has you!**

How do you develop a friendship? You know: spend time together. We've mentioned having devotional time with your mentee, but schedule fun times too: dates, walks, a swim, play golf or tennis, take in a movie, have lunch, call just to say, "Hi, how ya doin'?" Are you thinking, "Aren't I supposed to just teach them about God?" Exactly! **Jesus invited His mentees to be *with* Him. They "hung out" together.** They ministered together. (Mt 1:18-22, Mk 1:16-18, Lu. 5:1-11, Jn 1:37-39)

May I remind you that **God does not want to be Number One in your life? . . . God wants to BE your life.** (See Day 18) Jesus is not "part" of your life; He IS your life and He wants to be the center of all your relationships. **We need to share God-filled life together.** This is how we nurture a friendship. Who will your new disciple go to when he or she blows it, a mentor or a friend? **As mentors, we need to earn trust as a true friend.** Grow in grace side by side. As you spend time together, your friendship will grow naturally. At first you may have to "make it happen," but your relationship will grow into "let it happen" as you show faithfulness. *A friend loves at all times. . .* (Prv 17:17) **Be faithful privately too, and keep lifting your friend to the Lord.** He is the one who *sticks closer than a brother.* (Prv 18:24)

Lord, You are faithful. Help me to be faithful too. You have given me the privilege of sharing in Your work. May (mentee's name here) _____ *grow and become a mentoring friend to another. Thank You.*

Other passages for your prayerful consideration:
Jn 13:34-35, 17:20-23; Rom 12:9-13; Gal 6:1-2

Journaling: What activities do you enjoy doing with another? Ask your mentee what he or she likes to do. Perhaps you'll enjoy new things together. Schedule an informal activity with your mentee-friend.

Day Forty-Seven:
I Need to Caution this New Believer:
Beware of Religion without Relationship!

Not everyone who says to Me, "Lord, Lord," will enter the kingdom of heaven, but only he who does the will of My Father Who is in heaven. Many will say to Me on that day, "Lord, Lord, did we not prophesy in Your Name, and in Your Name drive out demons and perform many miracles?" Then I will tell them plainly, "I never knew you. Away from Me you evildoers!" (Mt 7:21-23)

"Brothers, listen to me! Your gods are made of metal, wood, and stone! Do they answer you when you pray to them? No! Do you have a relationship with them? No! Do you know that they love you? No! These are worthless idols! The Living God wants connection with you! It is He Who has made everything you see!" Paul was preaching passionately in the Hall of Tyrannus in the city of Ephesus when suddenly a shrill scream filled the air. A man came tearing through the crowd. When he saw Paul, he stopped and glared at him, hissing and foaming at the mouth. Paul stared into the man's eyes. "Come out of him in the Name of Jesus!" The man threw himself on the ground. He was shaking all over. Then, he was still, like a dead man. Paul walked over to the man and laid his hand on his forehead. The man's eyelids flickered, and then opened. Paul took him by the hand and lifted him up. "Dear brother," Paul said to him, "the Lord Jesus Christ has made you whole." The man fell to his knees, holding onto Paul's legs. Paul looked at the crowd of people who were standing still with their mouths open. "Don't look at me as though I am something special," he said. "This man is whole because of the power of God which is manifest in the Name of His Son, Jesus Christ. This is the God that I've been telling you about. He requires that all men turn from their wicked ways and put their faith in His Son Who paid the penalty for sin because He loves you."

Many turned to Christ that day, but not all. In the crowd were the seven sons of Sceva, a Jewish chief priest. They murmured quietly among themselves as they walked away. "That was incredible!" declared the youngest. "Harrumph!" The oldest exclaimed. "We know God and His law!" They began to go through the city and the surrounding areas, and when they encountered someone with an evil spirit, they would say, "In the Name of Jesus Whom Paul preaches, I command you to come out."

One day the evil spirit answered them, "Jesus I know, and I know about Paul, but who are you?" Then the man who had the evil spirit jumped on them and overpowered them all. He gave them such a beating that they ran into the house naked and bleeding. (Acts 19 with a little interpretation)

I'm sure you recognize this story. Is it possible to drive out evil spirits and do miracles in the Name of Jesus without knowing Him? Evidently, it is! God's Word tells the story. But there is the warning from Jesus noted above. **Religion is powerful, and our enemy knows how to use it to deceive. God is looking for fruit that comes out of relationship with Him, not a religious formula.**

The Pharisees and Sadducees in the Bible scare me. Those guys knew God's Word, yet they were "blind guides," "whitewashed tombs," and "children of the devil!" (Mt 23; Jn 8) What's to prevent me from becoming a prideful religious hypocrite? Religiosity could sneak up on me. Proverbs 4:23 tells us to guard our hearts. **We bear God-honoring fruit only because of being connected to Jesus.** (Jn 15:1-8) Do you know what it means to pray in the "NAME" of Jesus? It means "in the character and authority of." It is He Who works through us, for His glory. The devil is sly. When he can't get in through the front door, he sneaks around to the back. **Beware of the pity pit and the pride pit.** No doubt, you have already fought temptation along this line. Warn your mentee.

Lord, renew us daily, and keep drawing us to Yourself. Without You, we can do nothing. Help us to seek You daily for empowerment to do Your work for Your glory alone. Thank You, Jesus.

Other passages for your prayerful consideration:
1 Cor 10:3-5; Eph 6:10-18; Heb 12:1-13

Journaling: Make two opposing lists entitled "RELIGION" and "RELATIONSHIP", and contrast them.

Day Forty-Eight:
How Does One Handle the Enemy?—
His Pats on the Back ... Temptation ...

Humble yourselves, therefore, under God's mighty hand, that He may lift you up in due time. . . .Be self-controlled and alert. Your enemy the devil prowls around like a roaring lion looking for someone to devour. Resist him, standing firm in the faith. . . . (1 Pt 5:6-9)

"My Dear Wormwood,
    I note with great displeasure that your patient has become a Christian. Do not indulge in the hope that you will escape the usual penalties, indeed, in your better moments I trust that you would hardly wish to do so. In the meantime, we must make the best of the situation. There is no need to despair; hundreds of these adult converts have been reclaimed after a brief sojourn in the Enemy's camp and are now with us. All the habits of the patient, both mental and bodily, are still in our favour. . . . .
    Your affectionate uncle, Screwtape"
—from *The Screwtape Letters* (Lewis and Lewis 1981)

I have heard that a lion will simply bound forward and pounce on a young fawn. But, when stalking a mature buck, it will crawl on its belly up to one hundred yards, getting as close as possible in stealth before striking. Lewis said he had a hard time writing *"Screwtape"* because he had to think like the devil. I highly recommend this book and anything written by C. S. Lewis. **Our adversary is beaten by the life, death, and resurrection of our Lord and Savior, Jesus Christ.** However, Christ and His Church still have to deal with him. Make no mistake; Satan is real. He wants to see us in hell, but before that, to suffer and be separated from God, forever!

The *accuser of the brethren* (Rv 12:10) will come against us in any way he can; when one avenue fails, he will try another. For most of us, the outward sins fall away relatively quickly, and **the real battle is waged in the mind. The deeper sin nature includes fear, pride, lust, greed, envy, and indifference.** These feed the more recognizable "sins" – immorality, abuse of alcohol, drugs, money, and power, etc. That's why the Scripture exhorts us to allow our minds to be transformed. (Rom 12:1-2; Phil 2:5)

We dealt with self-righteousness/religiosity yesterday and tried to show how it can sneak up on us. Without realizing it, we've joined a "bless me" club, patting each other (and ourselves) on the back. The enemy is right there, also patting and whispering things like, "Yeah, you're a pretty good Christian." He can be very subtle.

Temptation comes to our flesh at our weakest points. If it is lust, opportunity to be unfaithful to God with our bodies will be attractively presented. If it's greed, unrighteous gain will knock on our door, and so on. **We must not only repent, but keep a repentant heart, so that God can be continually washing and strengthening**

us. This is true of direct temptation as well as "back door." Every successful resistance strengthens us, but if we're not careful, we can become self-assured and therefore vulnerable. In prayer, God will reveal the danger that the enemy is plotting. May I suggest asking God to reveal the end result of temptation? He will show you that *the wages of sin is death.* (Rom 6:23) Think and ask, "What would this do to my testimony for God? How would it affect my family? Would it really be worth all the pain? **Every sin grieves the heart of the Father (Ps 51: 1-17), Who gave His Son so that we could walk in victory!** But, it grieves Him more if we don't confess our sins and receive forgiveness and cleansing. (1 Jn 1:5 – 2:2) As you meditate on the passages noted on this page, think of how they can help your new disciple as well.

Father, the enemy has schemes. Help me to develop my own 'schemes' to be able to remain submitted to You and resist him. I want to honor you with all of my life, and to help _____ *to do the same. Thank You, Jesus.* (new disciple's name here)

Other passages for your prayerful consideration:
Gn 3:6, 4:6-7; 1 Jn 2:15-17; Jas 1:13-18

Journaling: Make a list of the strongest temptations you have. What have you done to combat them and keep from sinning? What do you do when you cross the line into sin? Are there other acts of repentance that would help you? Plan to walk your mentee through this process.

Day Forty-Nine:
Staying Focused: Growing a Disciple Who Will Grow Another

You will seek Me and find Me when you seek Me with all your heart.
(Jer 29:13)

"You mean he just left!?" The school at our church was new and small. We'd had a good first year. It was April, past time to be planning for the next year, and the principal was suddenly gone. I won't go into the details of why he departed, but he did so at a very difficult time. As the only Christian school educator on the board (I was teaching at another school), I offered to come over after school to just "stomp out the fires." When I checked with the staff, however, I found that nothing had been done in preparation for the next September. As God would have it, I was taking my second class in school administration at the university and needed a project. I threw all my energy, all that I knew, and what I was learning into enrollment for the next year. The plan had early success; almost 100% of that year's student body enrolled for fall. New students were coming in, too. By early summer, I estimated that we would need eight new classrooms! The school nearly doubled in size! By then, I had left my teaching position and become the principal. You may say, "You must have been focused," and I was, but more importantly, *God* was focused on that school. I simply stepped into His plan. I don't have space to tell you how many things had to fall into place. His hand on us was very evident. When we sought Him diligently and aligned our focus with His, much was accomplished.

A **focal point is a narrow thing by nature. It's not broad nor ambiguous. It's specific and clear.** That's why Jesus gave us the Great Commandments and the Great Commission in the Gospel of Matthew. (22:36-40 and 28:18-20) **What does He want us to do? In short, He wants us to love Him, love people, win the lost, and grow disciples.** That is the business of the Church and the individual members of it, His Body. **God wants us to devote ourselves to this common focus with our gifts, personalities, passions, and all that we are.** Nothing less satisfies. You know this, and the one you're mentoring needs to know it, too.

The central passage for the ministry of Win and Grow is 1 Pt 3:15. Let's look at it closely. *But in your hearts set apart Christ as Lord.* (I often hear this verse quoted without this first part, but it is the critical foundation for anything we do - the most important part of the passage.) Many people, things, and ideas vie for leadership in our lives, and some we must follow in a limited fashion. But Christ is set apart – pre-eminent. **His lordship is the singular litmus test that confirms all of our thoughts, actions, and words.** Next is the restatement of the Great Commission: *Always be prepared to give an answer to everyone who asks you to give the reason for the hope that you have.* There is a continuum in place. Some can't wait for those opportunities and are tempted to "make it happen." On the other end, some may think, "I hope nobody asks me anything. I wouldn't know what to say." The ministry of Win and Grow and this devotional and study guide is designed to help disciples at both ends and everyone in between. We hope and pray that as you complete this 50 days of devotion and study, you will find that any fear of sharing the Gospel with words, or by demonstrating God's love, is submitted to your heavenly Father. Each of us can <u>be prepared</u> with our own gifts, personalities, and passion, not someone else's! Finally, the passage tells us how to share: ***But do this with gentleness and respect.*** That's what we all want and need to do. No Bible thumping is called for, just a gentle and respectful witness, and **ALL** of us can do that. **We ALL can be ready when God opens the door to anyone who would receive God's message through us. You can model this for your new believer so that he/she, in turn, will one day become a mentor to someone else.**

Father, help me to get my eyes off of myself and onto You and Your commandments. I hope to teach others to do the same. Thank You that when I lose my focus, You make the picture clear again.

Other passages for your prayerful consideration:
Rom 10:8-15; 2 Cor 5:11-21; Heb 11:6, 12:1-3

Journaling: Go to 1 Peter 3:15. Write this passage in your own words. Personalize it by inserting your name. List some action steps that will help you to be and remain focused on embracing your gifts and fulfilling God's purpose. You may never be an "evangelist," but hopefully, you are no longer reluctant to share God's message.

Continually Feeding the Spring and Letting the Living Water Flow

Day Fifty:
Summing It All Up and Maintaining the Momentum

For I am the Lord, your God, who takes hold of your right hand and says to you, do not fear; I will help you. (Is 41:13) *And surely, I am with you always. . .* (Mt 28:20)

D ay 50, after Passover, was an important day in the Bible. It marked the beginning of the "Feast of Weeks" and was centered on the harvest of barley and wheat. Another name for this day that you'll likely know is "Pentecost." What a "harvest" of souls there was just ten days after Jesus ascended to heaven! The day was also called the "Day of First Fruits" because it was the time in which people were to bring offerings to God of the first fruits of their crops.

After His resurrection, Jesus appeared many times to the disciples over a period of forty days. At least once he was seen by over 500 brethren, many of whom were still alive in Paul's time. (1 Cor 15: 6). Just before He ascended into heaven, He told them to wait a few days to be baptized with the Holy Spirit. When this happened they would become His witnesses in Jerusalem, and in all Judea and Samaria, and to the ends of the earth. (Acts 1:1-11) This took place ten days later on Pentecost. (40 + 10 = 50)

Today, if you stayed on schedule, you are finishing fifty days in this devotional/ study guide as you read. **". . .You will be My witnesses. . . ." I'm sure that those early disciples had many different gifts and that most didn't have evangelism as a dominant gift, yet Jesus said this to ALL of them.** As you finish Day 50, may I encourage you to continue on your own? Let tomorrow be Day 51 and go right on to 365 as you live in and out of God's Word! Many great devotionals are full of nuggets of gold, but you will have gold nuggets of your own.

In His Steps is a best-selling book written by <u>Charles Monroe Sheldon</u>. (Sheldon 1921) It tells a story about a Reverend Henry Maxwell who challenges his congregation not to do anything for 365 days without first asking, "What Would Jesus Do?" It tells how they transformed their world. I highly recommend it as an inspiring read that shows what's possible with obedience to God. **The goal of Win and Grow Ministries and this tool, *THE RELUCTANT EVANGELIST: Embrace Your Gifts and Fulfill God's Purpose,* is to inspire, encourage, and equip you for a <u>lifetime</u>.** Our vision is to help develop sustainable ministry with individuals, churches, Christian schools, and other Christian communities. So, how do we **keep this ball rolling**?

1. **You, as a fully devoted follower of Jesus Christ (a disciple),** can use this book as a resource and a reminder of who you are in Christ and how He's made you to do your part in following the exhortation of 1 Pt 3:15. Some are using it to help mentor new believers.
2. If you did this with a church or another group of believers, you can decide to remain a Spirit-led and anointed worker with others under your leadership.
3. **If you are a leader of a group** who has used this resource for the last seven weeks, or if the Lord raised you up as a leader during this time, you want to think of where you've been, where you are now, and where your group is headed in the future.

Note: The people in your community are now more confident about sharing the gospel with their circles of influence and are committed to making disciples. How does this fact affect the ministry of your church in your community (your Jerusalem) and the world? What steps can be taken to keep everyone focused on the Great Commandments and the Great Commission?

Win and Grow is a "come along side" ministry, and we're committed to you. Contact information is at the bottom of the introduction. We are ready to help in the future in any way that we can.

He who goes out weeping, carrying seed to sow,
will return with songs of joy, carrying sheaves with him. **(Ps 126:6)**

Ask the Lord of the harvest. . .to send out workers
into His harvest field. **(Mt 9:38)**

Lord, thank you for how You have made me. You would not ask me to do what I cannot do in Your strength. Please help me to continuously set You apart in my heart as Lord and to be ready to share with anyone who asks about the hope that I have with gentleness and respect. (1 Pt 3:15)

Bibliography

2005. HOLY BIBLE, NEW INTERNATIONAL VERSION. Grand Rapids MI 49530: Zondervan

Barnhart, Clarence Lewis, Robert K. Barnhart, and World Book Inc. 1986. *The World Book dictionary*. 2 vols. Chicago: Published exclusively for World Book, Inc.

Blandy, Ernest W. 1890. Where He Leads Me Public Domain.

ChurchGrowth.org. "Free Spiritual Gifts Analysis." Church Growth Institute.

Hankey, Arabella K. 1866. I Love to Tell the Story. Public Domain.

Jessie. unknown. "Jesus Christ Takes Me Higher than any Drug Ever Could." [Testimony]. https://christianjourney.com/godsword/testimonyteen.html.

Lewis, C. S. *The chronicles of Narnia*: Macmillan.

Lewis, C. S., and C. S. Lewis. 1981. *The Screwtape letters; with, Screwtape proposes a toast*. Garden City, N.Y.: Image Books.

Rees, Erik. 2006. *S.H.A.P.E.: finding & fulfilling your unique purpose for life*. Grand Rapids, Mich.: Zondervan.

Schlemon, Alan. 2010. The Ambassador's Guide to Islam. Signal Hill, CA: Stand to Reason.

Sheldon, Charles Monroe. 1921. *In His steps to-day. What would Jesus do in solving the problems of present political, economic and social life?* New York, Chicago,: Fleming H. Revell Co.

unknown. The B-I-B-L-E. Public Domain.

Warren, Richard. 2002. *The purpose-driven life: what on earth am I here for?* Grand Rapids, Mich.: Zondervan.

Westcott, Brooke Foss, and Fenton John Anthony Hort. 1969. *The Kingdom inter-linear translation of the Greek Scriptures. Produced by New World Bible Translation Committee*: Brooklyn, Watchtower Bible and Tract Society of New York| 1969.

|1st ed. Non-fiction.

www.Barna.org. 2004. "Evangelism Is Most Effective Among Kids."

About Win and Grow Ministries

Win and Grow Helps All Christians to Be More Effective Disciple Makers

The **PURPOSE of WIN AND GROW** is to help all Christians become Disciple Makers.

The **VISION** of WIN AND GROW is to nurture every believer's God-given passion for souls so that they can share their faith naturally, using their own gifts and personalities.

The **FOCUS** of WIN AND GROW is on the 95% of those believers who do not have evangelism as a dominant gift but have passion to use their gifts to share the gospel when God opens the doors.

The **METHOD** of WIN AND GROW is to come alongside your community and help everyone to get personally engaged in outreach and discipleship, based on 1 Peter 3:15.

In your hearts set apart Christ as Lord. Always be prepared to give an answer to everyone who asks you to give the reason for the hope that you have. But do this with gentleness and respect.

How Does Win and Grow Work with Your Community?

We will engage with your leadership to tailor a plan that will address your needs.

Week 1: Assess your needs and develop a plan with you.

Weeks 2-8: Implement the 50-Day plan with the Whole Body.

Day 50: On Day 50, we'll gather with the leadership again including those developed during our time with you. We will celebrate our accomplishments and discuss how to keep the ball rolling. Our objective is to develop <u>sustainable</u> ministry. We'll be available to you after the 50 days.

Our Materials: *THE RELUCTANT EVANGELIST: Embrace Your Gifts and Fulfill God's Purpose* has been developed with over 40 years of research, study, and experience. It is a 50-Day devotional/study guide designed to help every believer focus their own passion, spiritual gifts, and personality to obey the Great Commandments and to be part of the fulfillment of the Great Commission.

Dave Kachele: (626) 905-2893 <u>WinNGrow@gmail.com</u> <u>www.winandgrow.com.</u> Facebook Twitter LinkedIn

About the Author

D ave Kachele holds a Bachelor of Science in Business Administration and teaching endorsement from University of Nevada, Las Vegas, and has served as teacher and administrator in Christian Schools for 30 years. He is ordained with the Association of Evangelical Gospel Assemblies, but is passionate that every believer in Christ is a leader and teacher of others. Since coming to Christ in 1974, he has been active in sharing the gospel of Jesus Christ, and helping people see themselves as positive witnesses of Christ, no matter what vocation, personality or stage of life they are in. He is father of four, grandfather of eight, and resides in Azusa, California with his wife, Dona.

For Further Reading

There are so many resources (human included) that have benefited me over the last 40+ years that I could not begin to list them all. I have deep appreciation for all the pastors, mentors, and other co-laborers that have helped me on my journey thus far, as well as all those in my future.

Below is a list of resources that will help you to grow further in the knowledge and grace of our Lord Jesus Christ. As you work in the Lord's harvest, I trust that you will find many more.

1. *HOW TO INFLUENCE YOUR LOVED ONES FOR CHRIST WHEN YOU DON'T HAVE THE GIFT OF EVANGELISM* by Larry Gilbert, Ephesians Four Ministries, Church Growth Institute, 1991, 1992, 1993, 1995, 1996, 2001, 2003. ISBN 0-941005-35-6. This book is included in the "Team Evangelism" materials, so it is written to fit within a program. However, the content provides an excellent tool for those who don't have the gift of evangelism but want to share their faith more effectively.

2. *HOW TO GIVE AWAY YOUR FAITH* by Paul Little, InterVarsity Press, 1966, 1988, and 2006. ISBN-10 0-8308-3406-0, ISBN-13 978-0-8308-3406-8. This book is a standard in the genre of sharing the gospel. It's timeless, excellent in "how to's," but also rich in encouragement on how to keep "feeding the spring," i.e. staying connected to Jesus.

3. *TACTICS* by Gregory Koukl, Zondervan, 2009. ISBN 978-0-310-28292-1. This book will teach you how to maneuver in conversations comfortably and graciously as you share your faith. It will give you a game plan for communicating with confidence and grace, even if you don't have the gift of evangelism.

4. *THE AMBASSADOR'S GUIDE TO Islam,* by Alan Shlemon, Stand to Reason, www.str.org This little booklet is an excellent tool for witnessing to Muslims. It shows you how to use the Qur'an to affirm the authority of the Bible.

5. *THE HOLE IN OUR GOSPEL* by Richard Stearns, World Vision. This was the 2010 Christian book of the year. This prophetic word to the Body of

Christ challenges us to demonstrate the gospel. The message in words will be unfruitful without showing the love of Jesus.

6. *GOD HAS A WONDERFUL PLAN FOR YOUR LIFE: The MYTH of the Modern Message* by Ray Comfort. This book explains why 80-90% of those making decisions for Christ fall away from the faith, and shows us how to include "the law" in our message to bring conviction before true repentance and lasting conversion.

7. *LIVING PROOF: Sharing the Gospel Naturally* by Jim Petersen, NAVPRESS, 1991. ISBN 08910-95616. This book will show you how to develop relationships with unreached people, model the Christian message, and present the Bible's claims in a non-threatening manner.

8. *THE CASE FOR CHRIST: A Journalist's Personal Investigation of the Evidence for Jesus* by Lee Strobel. Is there evidence that Jesus of Nazareth is the Son of God? Lee Strobel says there is, and *The Case For Christ* presents the evidence discovered during his two-year journey from atheism to faith as he sought to prove the claims of Christianity to be false.

9. **A GRACE DISGUISED: How the Soul Grows Through Loss** by Jerry Sittser, Zondervan, 1995. ISBN 0-310-21931-0. This book will help you understand your own loss and that of others with whom you will come into contact. It is available with more recent copyright dates.

10. *RANDOM DESIGNER: Created from Chaos to Connect with the Creator* by Richard G. Colling, PH.D. This book will help you to integrate science and faith and provides insight about how to talk with those who may have rejected faith on the basis of scientific discovery.

11. *KINGDOM OF THE CULTS* by Dr. Walter Martin has been recently updated. Bethany House. ISBN 0764228218. This book offers excellent information about and has keys for witnessing to people in cults such as Mormons and Jehovah's Witnesses.

12. *OIKOS: Your World Delivered*, by Tom Mercer, pastor of High Desert Church in Southern California, Professional Press, 2009, 2010. ISBN: 978-1-57087-709-4. This book encourages believers to share the gospel naturally in their own circles of influence.

13. *THE PURPOSE DRIVEN LIFE: What on earth am I here for?* by Rick Warren, Zondervan, 2002. ISBN 0-310-20571-9. This book helps believers to focus on God, their relationship with Him, and how to make His purpose their own.

14. *S.H.A.P.E.* by Erik Rees. Zondervan, 2006. ISBN 978-0-310-29248-7. This book will help you tap into the secrets of your own personal make-up.

15. *THE MARK OF A CHRISTIAN* by Francis Schaeffer, L'Abri Fellowship. InterVarsity Press, 1970. ISBN 0-87784-434-8. This classic shows how love and unity in the at-large Body of Christ is essential if the world is to believe the message of salvation by grace through faith.

16. *MAKING SPIRITUAL PROGRESS: Building Your Life with Faith, Hope, and Love* by Allen Ratta. InterVarsity Press, ISBN 978-0-8308-4405-0 (print)

ISBN 978-8308-6499-7 (digital). This book provides a monitoring system for your basic Christian motivations: Faith, Hope, and Love, providing a clear path for spiritual growth.

Websites for organizations which may help you in your desire to obey the Great Commandments and fulfill the Great Commission:

aega.org—Are you in full time ministry and not yet licensed? AEGA (the Association of Evangelical Gospel Assemblies) can help. They are an international group of independent ministers and ministries, and they will license even those of us who "fall through the cracks" of the normal denominational, Bible college route. Along with recognition of your calling, they provide many services including a Bible College that is fully accredited with Transworld Accreditation. AEGA can also help you set up your 501 (c) (3) non-profit ministry. Check them out.

wmpress.org—For FREE copies of partial books of scripture with study guides, gospel messages, and more go to this site.

http://churchgrowth.org Here's a site where you can get a FREE Spiritual Gifts assessment.

http://StrongFamilies.com Dr. John Trent has written many books including the best seller, *The Blessing*.

www.ptl.org The Pocket New Testament League has training and resources to help you share the Gospel

www.jewsforjesus.org This is a great place to find help with witnessing to your Jewish friends

www.lifeway.com This ministry provided the Spiritual Gifts Survey in this appendix

www.SpiritualProgress.com On-line tools to complement *MAKING SPIRITUAL PROGRESS*

Appendix A

Abbreviations used in this book for the books of the Old and New Testament

Old Testament

Gn	Genesis	2 Chr	2 Chronicles	Dn	Daniel
Ex	Exodus	Ezr	Ezra	Hos	Hosea
Lv	Leviticus	Neh	Nehemiah	Jl	Joel
Nm	Numbers	Est	Esther	Am	Amos
Dt	Deuteronomy	Jb	Job	Ob	Obadiah
Jo	Joshua	Ps	Psalms	Jon	Jonah
Jgs	Judges	Prv	Proverbs	Mi	Micah
Ru	Ruth	Eccl	Ecclesiastes	Na	Nahum
1 Sm	1 Samuel	Sg	Song of Songs	Hb	Habakkuk
2 Sm	2 Samuel	Is	Isaiah	Zep	Zephaniah
1 Kgs	1 Kings	Jer	Jeremiah	Hg	Haggai
2 Kgs	2 Kings	Lam	Lamentations	Zec	Zechariah
1 Chr	1 Chronicles	Ez	Ezekiel	Mal	Malachi

New Testament

Mt	Matthew	Eph	Ephesians	Heb	Hebrews
Mk	Mark	Phil	Philippians	Jas	James
Lk	Luke	Col	Colossians	1 Pt	1 Peter
Jn	John	1 Thes	1 Thessalonians	2 Pt	2 Peter
Acts	Acts	2 Thes	2 Thessalonians	1 Jn	1 John
Rom	Romans	1 Tm	1 Timothy	2 Jn	2 John
1 Cor	1 Corinthians	2 Tm	2 Timothy	3 Jn	3 John
2 Cor	2 Corinthians	Ti	Titus	Jude	Jude
Gal	Galatians	Phlm	Philemon	Rv	Revelation

Appendix B

Spiritual Gifts Survey

Lifeway Christian Resources, © 2003
used by permission

Discover Your Spiritual Gifts!
by Gene Wilkes

K en Hemphill defines a spiritual gift as "an individual manifestation of grace from the Father that enables you to serve Him and thus play a vital role in His plan for the redemption of the world."[1] Peter Wagner defines a spiritual gift as "a special attribute given by the Holy Spirit to every member of the Body of Christ according to God's grace for use within the context of the Body."[2] I like to use this definition:

> *Spiritual gifts are expressions of the Holy Spirit in the lives of believers which empowers them to serve the Body of Christ, the Church.*

Romans 12:6-8; 1 Corinthians 12:8-10, 28-30; Ephesians 4:11; and 1 Peter 4:9-11 contain representative lists of gifts and roles God has given to the church. A definition of these gifts follows.[3]

- **Leadership**—Leadership aids the body by leading and directing members to accomplish the goals and purposes of the church. Leadership motivates people to work together in unity toward common goals (Rom. 12:8).

- **Administration**—Persons with the gift of administration lead the body by steering others to remain on task. Administration enables the body to organize according to God-given purposes and long-term goals (1 Cor. 12:28).

- **Teaching**—Teaching is instructing members in the truths and doctrines of God's Word for the purposes of building up, unifying, and maturing the body (1 Cor. 12:28; Rom. 12:7; Eph. 4:11).

- **Knowledge**—The gift of knowledge manifests itself in teaching and training in discipleship. It is the God-given ability to learn, know, and explain the precious truths of God's Word. A word of knowledge is a Spirit-revealed truth (1 Cor. 12:28).

- **Wisdom**—Wisdom is the gift that discerns the work of the Holy Spirit in the body and applies His teachings and actions to the needs of the body (1 Cor. 12:28).

- **Prophecy**—The gift of prophecy is proclaiming the Word of God boldly. This builds up the body and leads to conviction of sin. Prophecy manifests itself in preaching and teaching (1 Cor. 12:10; Rom. 12:6).

- **Discernment**—Discernment aids the body by recognizing the true intentions of those within or related to the body. Discernment tests the message and actions of others for the protection and well-being of the body (1 Cor. 12:10).

- **Exhortation**—Possessors of this gift encourage members to be involved in and enthusiastic about the work of the Lord. Members with this gift are good counselors and motivate others to service. Exhortation exhibits itself in preaching, teaching, and ministry (Rom. 12:8).

- **Shepherding**—The gift of shepherding is manifested in persons who look out for the spiritual welfare of others. Although pastors, like shepherds, do care for members of the church, this gift is not limited to a pastor or staff member (Eph. 4:11).

- **Faith**—Faith trusts God to work beyond the human capabilities of the people. Believers with this gift encourage others to trust in God in the face of apparently insurmountable odds (1 Cor. 12:9).

- **Evangelism**—God gifts his church with evangelists to lead others to Christ effectively and enthusiastically. This gift builds up the body by adding new members to its fellowship (Eph. 4:11).

- **Apostleship**—The church sends apostles from the body to plant churches or be missionaries. Apostles motivate the body to look beyond its walls in order to carry out the Great Commission (1 Cor. 12:28; Eph. 4:11).

- **Service/Helps**—Those with the gift of service/helps recognize practical needs in the body and joyfully give assistance to meeting those needs. Christians with this gift do not mind working behind the scenes (1 Cor. 12:28; Rom. 12:7).

- **Mercy**—Cheerful acts of compassion characterize those with the gift of mercy. Persons with this gift aid the body by empathizing with hurting members. They keep the body healthy and unified by keeping others aware of the needs within the church (Rom. 12:8).

- **Giving**—Members with the gift of giving give freely and joyfully to the work and mission of the body. Cheerfulness and liberality are characteristics of individuals with this gift (Rom. 12:8).

- **Hospitality**—Those with this gift have the ability to make visitors, guests, and strangers feel at ease. They often use their home to entertain guests. Persons with this gift integrate new members into the body (1 Pet. 4:9).

God has gifted you with an expression of His Holy Spirit to support His vision and mission of the church. It is a worldwide vision to reach all people with the gospel of Christ. As a servant leader, God desires that you know how He has gifted you. This will lead you to where He would have you serve as part of His vision and mission for the church.

Gene Wilkes is pastor of the Legacy Drive Baptist Church, Plano, Texas. This article was adapted from *Jesus on Leadership* by Gene Wilkes (LifeWay Christian Resources 1998).

[1]Ken Hemphill, *Serving God: Discovering and Using Your Spiritual Gifts Workbook* (Dallas: The Sampson Company, 1995), 22. This product is distributed by and available from LifeWay Christian Resources of the Southern Baptist Convention, and may be purchased by calling toll free 1-800-458- 2772.

[2] *Your Spiritual Gifts Can Help Your Church Grow* by C. Peter Wagner, Copyright © 1979, Regal Books, Ventura, CA 93003. Used by permission, 42.

[3]These definitions exclude the "sign gifts" because of some confusion that accompanies these gifts and because they are difficult to fit into ministries within a typical church's ministry base.

SPIRITUAL GIFTS SURVEY DIRECTIONS

This is not a test, so there are no wrong answers. The *Spiritual Gifts Survey* consists of 80 statements. Some items reflect concrete actions; other items are descriptive traits; and still others are statements of belief.

- Select the one response you feel best characterizes yourself and place that number in the blank provided. Record your answer in the blank beside each item.
- Do not spend too much time on any one item. Remember, it is not a test. Usually your immediate response is best.
- Please give an answer for each item. Do not skip any items.
- Do not ask others how they are answering or how they think you should answer.
- Work at your own pace.

Your response choices are:
5—Highly characteristic of me/definitely true for me
4—Most of the time this would describe me/be true for me
3—Frequently characteristic of me/true for me–about 50 percent of the time
2—Occasionally characteristic of me/true for me–about 25 percent of the time
1—Not at all characteristic of me/definitely untrue for me

SPIRITUAL GIFTS SURVEY

_____1. I have the ability to organize ideas, resources, time, and people effectively.
_____2. I am willing to study and prepare for the task of teaching.
_____3. I am able to relate the truths of God to specific situations.
_____4. I have a God-given ability to help others grow in their faith.
_____5. I possess a special ability to communicate the truth of salvation.
_____6. I have the ability to make critical decisions when necessary.
_____7. I am sensitive to the hurts of people.
_____8. I experience joy in meeting needs through sharing possessions.
_____9. I enjoy studying.
_____10. I have delivered God's message of warning and judgment.
_____11. I am able to sense the true motivation of persons and movements.
_____12. I have a special ability to trust God in difficult situations.
_____13. I have a strong desire to contribute to the establishment of new churches.
_____14. I take action to meet physical and practical needs rather than merely talking about or planning to help.
_____15. I enjoy entertaining guests in my home.
_____16. I can adapt my guidance to fit the maturity of those working with me.
_____17. I can delegate and assign meaningful work.
_____18. I have an ability and desire to teach.
_____19. I am usually able to analyze a situation correctly.

156

_____20. I have a natural tendency to encourage others.

_____21. I am willing to take the initiative in helping other Christians grow in their faith.

_____22. I have an acute awareness of the emotions of other people, such as loneliness, pain, fear, and anger.

_____23. I am a cheerful giver.

_____24. I spend time digging into facts.

_____25. I feel that I have a message from God to deliver to others.

_____26. I can recognize when a person is genuine/honest.

_____27. I am a person of vision (a clear mental portrait of a preferable future given by God). I am able to communicate vision in such a way that others commit to making the vision a reality.

_____28. I am willing to yield to God's will rather than question and waver.

_____29. I would like to be more active in getting the gospel to people in other lands.

_____30. It makes me happy to do things for people in need.

_____31. I am successful in getting a group to do its work joyfully.

_____32. I am able to make strangers feel at ease.

_____33. I have the ability to plan learning approaches.

_____34. I can identify those who need encouragement.

_____35. I have trained Christians to be more obedient disciples of Christ.

_____36. I am willing to do whatever it takes to see others come to Christ.

_____37. I am attracted to people who are hurting.

_____38. I am a generous giver.

_____39. I am able to discover new truths.

_____40. I have spiritual insights from Scripture concerning issues and people that compel me to speak out.

_____41. I can sense when a person is acting in accord with God's will.

_____42. I can trust in God even when things look dark.

_____43. I can determine where God wants a group to go and help it get there.

_____44. I have a strong desire to take the gospel to places where it has never been heard.

_____45. I enjoy reaching out to new people in my church and community.

_____46. I am sensitive to the needs of people.

_____47. I have been able to make effective and efficient plans for accomplishing the goals of a group.

_____48. I often am consulted when fellow Christians are struggling to make difficult decisions.

_____49. I think about how I can comfort and encourage others in my congregation.

_____50. I am able to give spiritual direction to others.

_____51. I am able to present the gospel to lost persons in such a way that they accept the Lord and His salvation.

_____52. I possess an unusual capacity to understand the feelings of those in distress.

_____53. I have a strong sense of stewardship based on the recognition that God owns all things.

_____54. I have delivered to other persons messages that have come directly from God.

_____55. I can sense when a person is acting under God's leadership.

_____56. I try to be in God's will continually and be available for His use.

_____57. I feel that I should take the gospel to people who have different beliefs from me.

_____58. I have an acute awareness of the physical needs of others.

_____59. I am skilled in setting forth positive and precise steps of action.

_____60. I like to meet visitors at church and make them feel welcome.

_____61. I explain Scripture in such a way that others understand it.

_____62. I can usually see spiritual solutions to problems.

_____63. I welcome opportunities to help people who need comfort, consolation, encouragement, and counseling.

_____64. I feel at ease in sharing Christ with nonbelievers.

_____65. I can influence others to perform to their highest God-given potential.

_____66. I recognize the signs of stress and distress in others.

_____67. I desire to give generously and unpretentiously to worthwhile projects and ministries.

_____68. I can organize facts into meaningful relationships.

_____69. God gives me messages to deliver to His people.

_____70. I am able to sense whether people are being honest when they tell of their religious experiences.

_____71. I enjoy presenting the gospel to persons of other cultures and backgrounds.

_____72. I enjoy doing little things that help people.

_____73. I can give a clear, uncomplicated presentation.

_____74. I have been able to apply biblical truth to the specific needs of my church.

_____75. God has used me to encourage others to live Christ-like lives.

_____76. I have sensed the need to help other people become more effective in their ministries.

_____77. I like to talk about Jesus to those who do not know Him.

_____78. I have the ability to make strangers feel comfortable in my home.

_____79. I have a wide range of study resources and know how to secure information.

_____80. I feel assured that a situation will change for the glory of God even when the situation seems impossible.

SCORING YOUR SPIRITUAL GIFTS SURVEY

Follow these directions to figure your score for each spiritual gift.

1. Place in each box your numerical response (1-5) to the item number which is indicated below the box.
2. For each gift, add the numbers in the boxes and put the total in the TOTAL box.

LEADERSHIP	___ +	___ +	___ +	___ +	___ =	___
	Item 6	Item 16	Item 27	Item 43	Item 65	**TOTAL**
ADMINISTRATION	___ +	___ +	___ +	___ +	___ =	___
	Item 1	Item 17	Item 31	Item 47	Item 59	**TOTAL**
TEACHING	___ +	___ +	___ +	___ +	___ =	___
	Item 2	Item 18	Item 33	Item 61	Item 73	**TOTAL**
KNOWLEDGE	___ +	___ +	___ +	___ +	___ =	___
	Item 9	Item 24	Item 39	Item 68	Item 79	**TOTAL**
WISDOM	___ +	___ +	___ +	___ +	___ =	___
	Item 3	Item 19	Item 48	Item 62	Item 74	**TOTAL**
PROPHECY	___ +	___ +	___ +	___ +	___ =	___
	Item 10	Item 25	Item 40	Item 54	Item 69	**TOTAL**
DISCERNMENT	___ +	___ +	___ +	___ +	___ =	___
	Item 11	Item 26	Item 41	Item 55	Item 70	**TOTAL**
EXHORTATION	___ +	___ +	___ +	___ +	___ =	___
	Item 20	Item 34	Item 49	Item 63	Item 75	**TOTAL**
SHEPHERDING	___ +	___ +	___ +	___ +	___ =	___
	Item 4	Item 21	Item 35	Item 50	Item 76	**TOTAL**
FAITH	___ +	___ +	___ +	___ +	___ =	___
	Item 12	Item 28	Item 42	Item 56	Item 80	**TOTAL**
EVANGELISM	___ +	___ +	___ +	___ +	___ =	___
	Item 5	Item 36	Item 51	Item 64	Item 77	**TOTAL**
APOSTLESHIP	___ +	___ +	___ +	___ +	___ =	___
	Item 13	Item 29	Item 44	Item 57	Item 7	**TOTAL**
SERVICE/HELPS	___ +	___ +	___ +	___ +	___ =	___
	Item 14	Item 30	Item 46	Item 58	Item 72	**TOTAL**
MERCY	___ +	___ +	___ +	___ +	___ =	___
	Item 7	Item 22	Item 37	Item 52	Item 66	**TOTAL**
GIVING	___ +	___ +	___ +	___ +	___ =	___
	Item 8	Item 23	Item 38	Item 53	Item 67	**TOTAL**
HOSPITALITY	___ +	___ +	___ +	___ +	___ =	___
	Item 15	Item 32	Item 45	Item 60	Item 78	**TOTAL**

GRAPHING YOUR SPIRITUAL GIFTS PROFILE

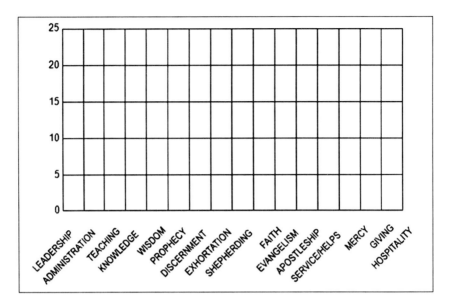

1. For each gift place a mark across the bar at the point that corresponds to your TOTAL for that gift.
2. For each gift shade the bar below the mark that you have drawn.
3. The resultant graph gives a picture of your gifts. Gifts for which the bars are tall are the ones in which you appear to be strongest. Gifts for which the bars are very short are the ones in which you appear not to be strong.

Now that you have completed the survey, thoughtfully answer the following questions.

The top three gifts I have begun to discover in my life are:

1. _____

2. _____

3. _____

- After prayer and worship, I am beginning to sense that God wants me to use my spiritual gifts to serve Christ's body by._____
- I am not sure yet how God wants me to use my gifts to serve others. But I am committed to prayer and worship, seeking wisdom and opportunities to use the gifts I have received from God.

Ask God to help you know how He has gifted you for service and how you can begin to use this gift in ministry to others.

Appendix C

Personality Assessment

Lion, Otter, Golden Retriever, Beaver:
Dr. John Trent

Instructions: Circle the descriptive words with which you identify in all squares. Double the number circled in each square. Mark a dot on the appropriate vertical line on the chart at the bottom: 1 dot for "L," "O," "G," and "B." Connect the dots. You have a graph that describes your personality. On the next page is an analysis of each personality type with help to move towards balance. (Used with permission.)

LOGB Strengths Assessment* Dr. John Trent

Takes charge	Bold
Determined	Purposeful
Assertive	Decision maker
Firm	Leader
Enterprising	Goal-driven
Competitive	Self-reliant
Enjoys challenges	Adventurous

"Let's do it now!"

Double the number circled _____

Takes risks	Fun-loving
Visionary	Likes variety
Motivator	Enjoys change
Energetic	Creative
Very verbal	Group-oriented
Promoter	Mixes easily
Avoids details	Optimistic

"Trust me! It'll work out!"

Double the number circled _____

Loyal	Adaptable
Nondemanding	Sympathetic
Even keel	Thoughtful
Avoids conflict	Nurturing
Enjoys routine	Patient
Dislikes change	Tolerant
Deep relationships	Good listener

"Let's keep things the way they are."

Double the number circled _____

Deliberate	Discerning
Controlled	Detailed
Reserved	Analytical
Predictable	Inquisitive
Practical	Precise
Orderly	Persistent
Factual	Scheduled

"How was it done in the past?"

Double the number circled _____

Strengths Assessment Chart

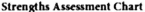
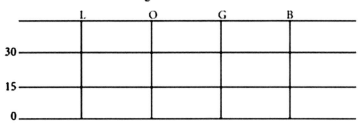

	L	O	G	B
30				
15				
0				

Personality Type Analysis

Each of us has these personality strengths in combinations which are variable and adjustable. They need to be brought into balance. Therefore, the goal is to honor your personality strengths and help you understand where you are "out of balance" in terms of your personality. We've found that our greatest personal strengths—when pushed out of balance—become our greatest weakness. For instance, let's say that your strength is that you have tremendous enthusiasm; this becomes a weakness as your enthusiasm turns into manipulation or obnoxious behavior. You can decide to decrease that trait and increase the characteristics of other traits. Let's take a closer look at four different personality types.

	The Captain (Lion)	The Social Director (Otter)	The Steward (Golden Retriever)	The Navigator (Beaver)
Relational Strengths:	Takes charge. Problem solver. Competitive. Enjoys change. Confrontational.	Optimistic. Energetic. Motivators. Future oriented.	Warm & Relational. Loyal. Enjoys Routine. Peace-Maker. Sensitive Feelings.	Accurate and precise. Quality control. Discerning. Analytical.
Strengths Out of Balance:	Too direct or impatient. Too busy. Cold blooded. Impulsive or takes big risks. Insensitive to others.	Unrealistic or day-dreamer. Impatient or over bearing. Manipulator or pushy. Avoids details or lacks follow-through.	Attract the hurting. Missed opportunities. Stays in a rut. Sacrifice own feelings for harmony. Easily hurt or holds a grudge.	Too critical or too strict. Too controlling. Too negative of new opportunities. Lose overview.
Communi-cation Style:	Direct or blunt. One-way. Weakness: Not as good a listener.	Can inspire others. Optimistic or enthusiastic. One-way. Weakness: High energy can manipulate others.	Indirect. Two-way. Great listener. Weakness: Uses too many words or provides too many details.	Factual. Two-way. Great listener (tasks). Weakness: Desire for detail and precision can frustrate others.

Personality Type Analysis

Relational Needs:	Personal attention & recognition for what they do. Areas where he or she can be in charge. Opportunity to solve problems. Freedom to change. Challenging activities.	Approval. Opportunity to verbalize. Visibility. Social recognition.	Emotional security. Agreeable Environment.	Quality. Exact expectations.
Relational Balance:	Add softness. Become a great listener.	Be attentive to other's needs. There is such a thing as too much optimism.	Learn to say "NO" . . . establish emotional boundaries. Learn to confront when own feelings are hurt.	Total support is not always possible. Thorough explanation isn't everything.

164

CPSIA information can be obtained at www.ICGtesting.com
Printed in the USA
BVOW01s0313300115

385653BV00005B/13/P